P9-AOA-946

SPECTRUM®

Data Analysis and Probability

Grades 6–8

Published by Spectrum®
an imprint of Carson-Dellosa Publishing LLC
Greensboro, NC

Spectrum® is an imprint of Carson–Dellosa Publishing.

Printed in the United States of America. All rights reserved. Except as permitted under the United States Copyright Act, no part of this publication may be reproduced or distributed in any form or by any means, or stored in a database or retrieval system, without prior written permission from the publisher, unless otherwise indicated. Spectrum® is an imprint of Carson–Dellosa Publishing. © 2011 Carson–Dellosa Publishing.

Send all inquiries to:
Carson–Dellosa Publishing
P.O. Box 35665
Greensboro, NC 27425 USA

Printed in the USA

ISBN 978-0-7696-6316-6

04-238137811

Table of Contents Data Analysis and Probability

Chapter 1 Math for Data Analysis

Chapter 2 Algebra

Chapter 3 Graphing Ratios

Chapter 4 Probability

Chapter 5 Measures of Central Tendency

Chapter 6 Creating and Interpreting Graphs

NAME ____________________

Check What You Know

Math for Data Analysis

CHAPTER 1 PRETEST

Add, subtract, multiply, or divide. Write each answer in simplest form.

	a	b	c	d
1.	$\frac{1}{2} + \frac{3}{4}$	$2\frac{2}{3} + 1\frac{3}{5}$	$2\frac{5}{6} - \frac{2}{3}$	$9\frac{1}{6} - 7\frac{1}{4}$
2.	$\frac{3}{8} \times \frac{2}{3} =$ ____	$2\frac{2}{5} \times 2 \times 1\frac{1}{3} =$ ____	$\frac{3}{10} \div \frac{4}{5} =$ ____	$1\frac{2}{3} \div \frac{5}{9} =$ ____
3.	$2.9 + 3.2$	$5.04 + 3.635$	$8.23 - 6.4$	$5 - 1.256$
4.	8.5×3	0.43×2.2	0.7×0.008	2.853×3.3
5.	$3\overline{)4.8}$	$0.5\overline{)250}$	$0.02\overline{)0.826}$	$1.3\overline{)7.2618}$

NAME ________________________

CHAPTER 1 PRETEST

Check What You Know

Math for Data Analysis

Solve each problem.

6. Turner Paint Company has $9\frac{1}{3}$ vats of paint. Each vat holds $5\frac{1}{4}$ gallons of paint. How much paint does the company have?

Turner has ________ gallons of paint.

7. Tara has $14\frac{2}{3}$ square yards of fabric to make shirts. Each shirt requires $2\frac{3}{4}$ square yards of fabric. How many complete shirts can Tara make? How much fabric will be left over?

Tara can make ________ shirts.

Tara will have ________ square yard(s) left over.

8. Jamie bought a DVD that cost $14.99. Tax was 82 cents. How much did Jamie owe for the DVD? Jamie paid with a $20 bill. How much change did he receive?

Jamie owed ________.

Jamie received ________ in change.

9. Elan works at a call center. On average, Elan can handle 3.62 calls from customers per hour. How many calls can Elan handle in a $7\frac{1}{2}$ hour workday?

Elan can handle ________ calls in a workday.

10. On a particular day, Elan worked 8.25 hours and handled 34 calls. How many calls did Elan handle per hour that day? Round to hundredths.

Elan handled ________ calls per hour (rounded).

NAME ____________________

Lesson 1.1 Reducing to Simplest Form

Factors are numbers or expressions that multiply together to form a product. The factors in bold below are common to both 16 and 24. The greatest common factor is 8.

16 = 1 × 16, 2 × 8, 4 × 4 — **1**, **2**, **4**, **8**, and 16 are factors of 16

24 = 1 × 24, 2 × 12, 3 × 8, 4 × 6 — **1**, **2**, 3, **4**, 6, **8**, 12, and 24 are factors of 24

A fraction is in simplest form when the greatest common factor of the numerator and denominator is 1. To reduce a fraction to simplest form, divide the numerator and denominator by their greatest common factor.

$$\frac{6}{12} = \frac{6 \div 6}{12 \div 6} = \frac{1}{2} \qquad 7\frac{14}{21} = \frac{14 \div 7}{21 \div 7} = 7\frac{2}{3}$$

For each number, identify the factors, common factors, and greatest common factor.

		Factors	Common Factor(s)	Greatest Common Factor
1.	5	________		
	30	________	________	________
2.	10	________		
	20	________	________	________
3.	12	________		
	18	________	________	________

Write each of the following in simplest form.

	a	b	c
4.	$\frac{5}{30}$ ________	$\frac{10}{20}$ ________	$\frac{15}{18}$ ________
5.	$3\frac{8}{12}$ ________	$4\frac{6}{8}$ ________	$5\frac{6}{24}$ ________

NAME ______________________

Lesson 1.2 Finding Common Denominators

The least common multiple (LCM) is the smallest multiple that two numbers share. To find the LCM of two numbers, list several multiples of the larger number. Then, list multiples of the smaller number until you come to a shared multiple.

Multiples of 5 are 5, 10, 15, **20**, 25, and so on.

Multiples of 4 are 4, 8, 12, 16, **20**, and so on. The LCM of 4 and 5 is 20.

You can rename fractions so they have common denominators. Multiply the top and bottom of each fraction by the number that makes the denominator equal the LCM.

$\frac{1}{4}$ and $\frac{2}{5}$ do not have common denominators. The LCM of the denominators is 20.

$\frac{1}{4} \times \frac{5}{5} = \frac{5}{20}$ $\frac{2}{5} \times \frac{4}{4} = \frac{8}{20}$ $\frac{5}{20}$ and $\frac{8}{20}$ have common denominators.

Find the LCM and rename each pair of fractions with common denominators.

	a	b
1.	$\frac{1}{3}$ and $\frac{1}{4}$ ________	$\frac{3}{5}$ and $\frac{3}{8}$ ________
2.	$\frac{1}{2}$ and $\frac{7}{8}$ ________	$\frac{1}{6}$ and $\frac{1}{9}$ ________
3.	$\frac{3}{4}$ and $\frac{1}{10}$ ________	$\frac{2}{3}$ and $\frac{1}{6}$ ________
4.	$\frac{1}{7}$ and $\frac{3}{8}$ ________	$\frac{1}{2}$ and $\frac{3}{5}$ ________
5.	$\frac{3}{16}$ and $\frac{1}{4}$ ________	$\frac{3}{8}$ and $\frac{1}{6}$ ________

NAME ____________________

Lesson 1.3 Renaming Fractions and Mixed Numerals

Every whole number can be written as a fraction with a denominator of 1.

$$3 = \frac{3}{1} \qquad 10 = \frac{10}{1} \qquad 25 = \frac{25}{1}$$

Change $2\frac{3}{4}$ to a fraction.

$$2\frac{3}{4} = \frac{2}{1} + \frac{3}{4} = \frac{2 \times 4}{4} + \frac{3}{4}$$

$$= \frac{8 + 3}{4} = \frac{11}{4}$$

Change $\frac{15}{6}$ to a mixed numeral.

$$\frac{15}{6} = 2\frac{3}{6} = 2\frac{1}{2}$$

Change each of the following to a fraction. Reduce to simplest form.

	a	b	c	d
1.	$2\frac{3}{8}$ ______	4 ______	$3\frac{3}{8}$ ______	$1\frac{2}{4}$ ______
2.	$5\frac{1}{3}$ ______	$2\frac{3}{15}$ ______	$1\frac{5}{8}$ ______	23 ______
3.	$7\frac{3}{5}$ ______	$2\frac{2}{3}$ ______	$2\frac{4}{12}$ ______	$8\frac{3}{4}$ ______

Change each of the following to a mixed numeral in simplest form.

4.	$\frac{17}{8}$ ______	$\frac{37}{9}$ ______	$\frac{40}{10}$ ______	$\frac{14}{4}$ ______
5.	$6\frac{7}{5}$ ______	$\frac{15}{13}$ ______	$\frac{18}{8}$ ______	$\frac{150}{15}$ ______
6.	$2\frac{14}{12}$ ______	$\frac{25}{2}$ ______	$\frac{24}{14}$ ______	$\frac{12}{9}$ ______

NAME ________________________

Lesson 1.4 Adding and Subtracting Fractions

To add or subtract fractions when the denominators are different, rename the fractions so the denominators are the same.

$$\begin{array}{r}\frac{2}{3}\\ +\frac{3}{7}\\ \hline\end{array} = \begin{array}{r}\frac{2}{3}\times\frac{7}{7}\\ +\frac{3}{7}\times\frac{3}{3}\\ \hline\end{array} = \begin{array}{r}\frac{14}{21}\\ +\frac{9}{21}\\ \hline \frac{23}{21}\end{array} = 1\frac{2}{21}$$

$$\begin{array}{r}\frac{4}{5}\\ -\frac{1}{10}\\ \hline\end{array} = \begin{array}{r}\frac{4}{5}\times\frac{2}{2}\\ -\frac{1}{10}\\ \hline\end{array} = \begin{array}{r}\frac{8}{10}\\ -\frac{1}{10}\\ \hline \frac{7}{10}\end{array}$$

To add or subtract mixed numerals when the denominators of the fractions are different, find a common denominator and rename the fractions.

$$\begin{array}{r}3\frac{1}{2}\\ +2\frac{2}{3}\\ \hline\end{array} = \begin{array}{r}3\frac{3}{6}\\ +2\frac{4}{6}\\ \hline 5\frac{7}{6}\end{array} = 6\frac{1}{6}$$

$$\begin{array}{r}4\frac{1}{4}\\ -2\frac{5}{6}\\ \hline\end{array} = \begin{array}{r}4\frac{3}{12}\\ -2\frac{10}{12}\\ \hline\end{array} = \begin{array}{r}3\frac{15}{12}\\ -2\frac{10}{12}\\ \hline 1\frac{5}{12}\end{array}$$

Write each answer in simplest form.

	a	b	c	d
1.	$\frac{1}{3} + \frac{1}{5}$	$\frac{1}{6} + \frac{1}{2}$	$\frac{2}{3} - \frac{3}{8}$	$\frac{5}{6} - \frac{3}{4}$
2.	$1\frac{3}{4} + 4\frac{3}{8}$	$2\frac{7}{8} + 1\frac{1}{2}$	$4\frac{5}{6} - 4\frac{5}{8}$	$6\frac{7}{10} - 3\frac{4}{5}$

Use the table to solve the problems below.

Stock of Nuts at Jason's Market in pounds (lb.)	
Peanuts	$8\frac{7}{9}$ lb.
Cashews	$6\frac{2}{3}$ lb.
Almonds	$10\frac{5}{6}$ lb.

3. Jason's Market began the day with the stock of nuts listed in the table. During the day, customers bought $1\frac{2}{3}$ pounds of peanuts. How many pounds were left?

________ pounds of peanuts were left.

4. Jason's Market received a shipment of $4\frac{3}{4}$ pounds of cashews. How many pounds of cashews does the market now have in stock?

The market now has ________ pounds of cashews.

NAME ____________________

Lesson 1.5 Multiplying Fractions and Mixed Numerals

To multiply fractions, first reduce to simplest form. Then, multiply the numerators and multiply the denominators.

$$\frac{3}{5} \times \frac{5}{6} \times \frac{1}{7} = \frac{\overset{1}{\cancel{3}} \times 5 \times 1}{5 \times \underset{2}{\cancel{6}} \times 7} = \frac{1 \times 5 \times 1}{5 \times 2 \times 7} = \frac{5}{70}$$

To multiply mixed numerals, first rename the numbers as fractions. Reduce to simplest form. Then, multiply the numerators and multiply the denominators. Simplify the result.

$$3\frac{1}{5} \times 2\frac{2}{3} \times 1\frac{1}{8} = \frac{16 \times \overset{1}{\cancel{8}} \times \overset{3}{\cancel{9}}}{5 \times \underset{1}{\cancel{3}} \times \underset{1}{\cancel{8}}} = \frac{16 \times 1 \times 3}{5 \times 1 \times 1} = \frac{48}{5} = 9\frac{3}{5}$$

Write each answer in simplest form.

	a	b	c	d
1.	$\frac{3}{7} \times \frac{1}{2}$ ______	$\frac{5}{6} \times \frac{3}{4}$ ______	$\frac{4}{5} \times \frac{5}{12} \times \frac{1}{6}$ ______	$\frac{2}{3} \times \frac{1}{5} \times \frac{3}{10}$ ______
2.	$\frac{2}{3} \times \frac{1}{4} \times \frac{6}{8}$ ______	$\frac{4}{5} \times \frac{5}{8} \times \frac{3}{4}$ ______	$\frac{5}{6} \times 4\frac{1}{2} \times 2\frac{2}{3}$ ______	$2\frac{1}{4} \times \frac{2}{7} \times \frac{7}{8}$ ______

Complete the table.

Recipe for Ginger Cookies			
Ingredient	**Amount**	**Half the Recipe**	**$3\frac{1}{3}$ of the Recipe**
Butter	$\frac{3}{4}$ cup		
Sugar	$1\frac{1}{2}$ cups		
Flour	$3\frac{1}{8}$ cups		
Ginger	$2\frac{1}{4}$ teaspoons		

3. You want to make half the number of cookies this recipe will produce. Determine the amount of each ingredient you need. Write the amounts in the third column.

4. You decide to make $3\frac{1}{3}$ times the original recipe for the class bake sale. Write the amount of each ingredient in the fourth column.

NAME ____________________

Lesson 1.6 Dividing Fractions and Mixed Numerals

Any two numbers with a product of 1 are **reciprocals**.

$\frac{3}{4} \times \frac{4}{3} = \frac{12}{12} = 1$

$\frac{3}{4}$ and $\frac{4}{3}$ are reciprocals

$1\frac{3}{4} \times \frac{4}{7} = \frac{7}{4} \times \frac{4}{7} = \frac{28}{28} = 1$

$1\frac{3}{4}$ (or $\frac{7}{4}$) and $\frac{4}{7}$ are reciprocals

To divide by a fraction, multiply by its reciprocal.

$\frac{2}{3} \div \frac{5}{8} = \frac{2}{3} \times \frac{8}{5} = \frac{16}{15} = 1\frac{1}{15}$

$1\frac{2}{3} \div 2\frac{5}{9} = \frac{5}{\cancel{3}_1} \times \frac{\cancel{9}^3}{23} = \frac{15}{23}$

Write the reciprocal.

	a	b	c	d
1.	$\frac{3}{7}$ ________	$1\frac{1}{5}$ ________	29 ________	$2\frac{2}{9}$ ________

Write each answer in simplest form.

	a	b	c	d
2.	$\frac{3}{8} \div \frac{1}{4}$ ________	$2\frac{1}{5} \div 1\frac{1}{10}$ ________	$4\frac{1}{6} \div \frac{2}{3}$ ________	$3\frac{2}{7} \div 1\frac{5}{7}$ ________
3.	$6\frac{1}{3} \div 2\frac{1}{6}$ ________	$5 \div \frac{5}{8}$ ________	$2\frac{2}{9} \div \frac{5}{12}$ ________	$1\frac{1}{5} \div 2\frac{2}{3}$ ________
4.	$3\frac{1}{3} \div 4$	$\frac{3}{8} \div \frac{3}{4}$	$1\frac{7}{8} \div 2\frac{3}{4}$	$4\frac{1}{8} \div \frac{1}{16}$

5. A truck uses $4\frac{1}{10}$ gallons of gas to go $51\frac{1}{4}$ miles. How many miles per gallon does the truck get?

The truck gets ________ miles per gallon.

NAME ______________________________

Lesson 1.7 Converting Decimals and Fractions

Convert $\frac{2}{5}$ to tenths.
$\frac{2}{5} = \frac{2 \times 2}{5 \times 2} = \frac{4}{10} = 0.4$

Convert $\frac{3}{20}$ to hundredths.
$\frac{3}{20} = \frac{3 \times 5}{20 \times 5} = \frac{15}{100} = 0.15$

Convert $\frac{12}{25}$ to thousandths.
$\frac{12}{25} = \frac{12 \times 40}{25 \times 40} = \frac{480}{1{,}000} = 0.480$

Convert decimals to fractions or mixed numbers.

$0.6 = \frac{6}{10}$
$= \frac{3}{5}$

$2.25 = 2\frac{25}{100}$
$= 2\frac{1}{4}$

$1.875 = 1\frac{875}{1{,}000}$
$= 1\frac{7}{8}$

Convert each fraction to a decimal.

	a	b	c
	Convert to tenths.	Convert to hundredths.	Convert to thousandths.
1.	$\frac{1}{2}$ ________	$1\frac{3}{4}$ ________	$\frac{3}{50}$ ________
2.	$3\frac{2}{5}$ ________	$2\frac{3}{20}$ ________	$5\frac{15}{200}$ ________
3.	$4\frac{1}{5}$ ________	$5\frac{9}{10}$ ________	$4\frac{82}{250}$ ________

Convert to ten thousandths.

4.	$2\frac{839}{1{,}000}$ ________	$1\frac{96}{500}$ ________	$3\frac{2{,}046}{2{,}500}$ ________

Convert each decimal to a fraction or mixed numeral in simplest form.

5.	0.9 ________	3.5 ________	4.8 ________
6.	0.25 ________	2.45 ________	6.11 ________
7.	0.205 ________	1.888 ________	2.205 ________

NAME ______________________________

Lesson 1.8 Adding and Subtracting Decimals

When adding or subtracting decimals, keep the decimal points aligned. It may help to write in 0s as placeholders. Then, add or subtract decimals as you would whole numbers.

$$\begin{array}{r} 27.3824 \\ 1.437 \\ +\ 3.2169 \\ \hline 32.0363 \end{array} \quad \text{OR} \quad \begin{array}{r} 27.3824 \\ 1.4370 \\ +\ 3.2169 \\ \hline 32.0363 \end{array}$$

The zero was added to mark place value.

Add or subtract.

	a	b	c	d	e
1.	0.8 + 0.3	5.8 + 2.5	37.54 + 4.25	3.06 + 5.235	0.9372 + 0.383
2.	2.1 + 3.975	0.5723 + 0.822 + 0.51	5.0337 + 6.5542 + 2.4382	11.6 + 4.856 + 3.79	3.037 + 0.11 + 3.4687
3.	0.5 − 0.3	2.78 − 0.8	19.2 − 5.33	3.568 − 1.629	35.431 − 3.72

4. How much rain fell in Seattle during the five-year period shown in the table?

________ inches of rain fell.

5. How much more rain fell in Seattle in the wettest year than in the driest year?

________ more inches of rain fell.

Total Rainfall Seattle, Washington	
Year	**Inches**
2009	11.07
2008	9.38
2007	14.02
2006	16.38
2005	9.35

NAME ____________________

Lesson 1.9 Multiplying Decimals

When multiplying decimals, count the number of decimal places in each factor to figure out the placement of the decimal point in the product.

3	0.3	0.3	0.3
× 5	× 5	× 0.5	× 0.05
15	1.5	0.15	0.015
0 + 0 = 0	1 + 0 = 1	1 + 1 = 2	1 + 2 = 3
decimal places	decimal place	decimal places	decimal places

Multiply.

	a	**b**	**c**	**d**	**e**
1.	4.1 × 2	0.35 × 3	2.321 × 10	87.1 × 5	5.5 × 9.1
2.	15.03 × 8	3.16 × 4.2	3.36 × 0.3	2.743 × 1.1	0.3403 × 4
3.	4.9 × 3.07	2.44 × 0.005	0.09 × 0.002	2.566 × 1.21	1.08 × 1.032

4. Mika earns $11.30 per hour on her job. Overtime pay is 1.5 times regular pay. Mika agreed to work overtime this weekend. How much will she earn per hour?

Mika will earn ________ per hour.

5. A furniture manufacturer needs 21.6 yards of fabric to cover one couch. Each yard costs $14.15. How much does the fabric cost per couch?

The fabric costs ________ for each couch.

NAME ______________________

Lesson 1.10 Dividing Decimals

When you divide a decimal by any whole number, place the decimal point in the quotient directly above the decimal point in the dividend.

$$\begin{array}{r} 0.54 \\ 6\overline{)3.24} \\ -\,3\,0 \\ \hline 2\,4 \\ -\,2\,4 \\ \hline 0 \end{array}$$

When you divide a whole number by a decimal, multiply the divisor and dividend by 10, 100, or 1,000 so the new divisor is a whole number.

$$0.7\overline{)49} = \begin{array}{r} 70 \\ 7\overline{)490} \\ -\,490 \\ \hline 0 \end{array}$$

When you divide a decimal by a decimal, multiply the divisor and the dividend by the same power of 10 to change the divisor to a whole number.

$$1.05\overline{)2.415} = \begin{array}{r} 2.3 \\ 105\overline{)241.5} \\ -\,210 \\ \hline 31\,5 \\ -\,31\,5 \\ \hline 0 \end{array}$$

Divide.

	a	b	c	d
1.	$2\overline{)0.8}$	$5\overline{)2.25}$	$3\overline{)1.806}$	$8\overline{)0.1648}$
2.	$0.4\overline{)32}$	$1.2\overline{)144}$	$0.07\overline{)497}$	$0.006\overline{)36}$
3.	$1.8\overline{)44.1}$	$0.16\overline{)0.0512}$	$0.0009\overline{)27.9}$	$2.422\overline{)3.8752}$

NAME ____________________

Lesson 1.11 Designing a Study

Step 1: Ask a question
What do you want to learn from your study? Be specific! For example, you might want to know which brand of tomato soup is most nutritious. Your question might be: Which brand of tomato soup provides the most protein with the least fat?

Step 2: Identify your sample
Identify the population you want to study. A **population** is the set of all items of interest to your study. A population might be all students in your school or all brands of tomato soup offered for sale in your town.

You probably cannot collect data from every member of the population. Instead, you can collect data from a **sample**, or part of the population. The sample must accurately represent the whole population. You want to be able to draw conclusions about the population based on the sample. A sample is **biased** if it does not accurately represent the population. In the soup example, our sample might be all brands of tomato soup offered for sale at three stores in your community.

Step 3: Collect data
First, identify the data you want to collect. **Data** are items of information, such as facts or statistics. In our study, we want data on protein and fat.

Next, decide how to collect the data. If you want to gather information from people, you could write questions for members of your sample to answer. To gather data about soup, you might go to three stores. You would record all brands of tomato soup on the shelves and the amounts of protein and fat in each brand.

Step 4: Analyze data
Organize your data in a meaningful way, such as in a table. This table organizes grams of protein and fat in tomato soup.

Nutrition Facts about Tomato Soup
in grams (g)

Brand	Protein	Total Fat
X	5 g	2 g
Y	6 g	4 g
Z	2 g	1 g

How can you analyze this data to determine the answer to your question: Which brand provides the most protein with the least fat? One way is to use fractions to find the total fat per gram of protein in each brand. Then, convert the factions to decimals to make them easier to compare.

Brand X: 2 g fat/5 g protein = 0.4 g fat per gram of protein

Brand Y: 4 g fat/6 g protein = 0.7 g fat per gram of protein (rounded)

Brand Z: 1 g fat/2 g protein = 0.5 g fat per gram of protein

Step 5: Interpret results
From your analysis, you could conclude that Brand X is the most nutritious soup, because it contains the least fat per gram of protein.

NAME ______________________

Lesson 1.11 Designing a Study

Now, design your own study.

Step 1: Ask a question. What is the most popular ________ among males and females? You fill in the blank. For example, you might fill in *pet, color,* or *sport.*

Step 2: Identify your sample. Choose a sample of 20 people, 10 males and 10 females. You can include family, friends, and classmates.

Step 3: Collect data. List 4 choices within the category you chose. For example, if your category is *pet,* you might list cat, dog, snake, and bird. Design a survey form that lists the choices and asks people to rank them from 1 (least favorite) to 4 (most favorite). Include a way for people to identify themselves as male or female. Distribute the forms to each member of your sample. Collect the completed forms.

Step 4: Analyze data. List your 4 choices in the first column of the table below. Divide the surveys into those submitted by males and those submitted by females. Add the scores for the first choice from all males. Write this total in the first cell below *Males.* Add the scores for the second choice from all males. Write this total in the second cell under *Males.* After you complete the column for males, add scores for the *Females* column. Complete the *Total Score* column by totaling the scores across rows.

Which choice received the highest total score?

____

What fraction of this total score came from males?

____

What fraction of this total score came from females?

____

Popularity of ______________			
Choices	**Males**	**Females**	**Total Score**

Step 5: Interpret results. Write a one-sentence answer to your study question.

____

____

NAME ______________________

Check What You Learned

Math for Data Analysis

Add, subtract, multiply, or divide. Write each answer in simplest form.

	a	b	c	d
1.	$\frac{7}{8} + 2\frac{1}{6}$	$1\frac{2}{5} + 3\frac{2}{3}$	$\frac{3}{4} - \frac{1}{12}$	$4\frac{1}{18} - 3\frac{5}{6}$
2.	$\frac{5}{8} \times \frac{1}{5} =$ ______	$3\frac{3}{4} \times 4 \times 1\frac{1}{15} =$ ______	$4 \div \frac{3}{7} =$ ______	$3\frac{1}{8} \div 4\frac{1}{6} =$ ______
3.	3.98 + 1.66	0.556 + 1.7 + 0.68	8.324 − 6.8	3 − 2.805
4.	6.8 × 4.3	2.76 × 2.6	3.243 × 1.4	0.634 × 4.02
5.	$9\overline{)227.7}$	$2.6\overline{)91}$	$1.3\overline{)2.704}$	$0.02\overline{)5.836}$

NAME ______________________

Check What You Learned

Math for Data Analysis

CHAPTER 1 POSTTEST

Solve each problem.

6. On average, Murray Motors makes $9\frac{2}{5}$ car engines in an hour. The company wants to raise this average to $1\frac{1}{4}$ times this amount. How many engines does the company want to make per hour?

Murray Motors wants to make ________ engines per hour.

7. The Free Store has $12\frac{3}{8}$ pounds of cheese. The store wants to divide the cheese into $\frac{3}{4}$ pound portions to distribute to homeless people. How many portions will the cheese make?

The cheese will make ________ portions.

8. Tracy drives a bus. She drove 16.09 kilometers to her first stop, 14.372 kilometers to her second stop, and 7.5 kilometers to her third stop. How far did she drive?

Tracy drove ________ kilometers.

9. Sam bought a cell phone for $49.95. Sales tax in his state is 0.055 of the purchase price. How much did Sam pay for the phone? Round up.

Sam paid ________ for the cell phone.

10. Mario has $22.35 to spend on gasoline. Each gallon costs $2.69. How many gallons of gasoline can Mario buy? Round to tenths.

Mario can buy ________ gallons of gasoline.

NAME ____________________

Check What You Know

Algebra

CHAPTER 2 PRETEST

Identify the coefficient and the variable in each term below.

	a	b
1.	$12n$	d
	coefficient _____ variable _____	coefficient _____ variable _____

Write each item as an expression, equation, or inequality. Use n for an unknown number.

2. two 3s are less than n ____________________ the product of a number and 5 ____________________

Underline the operation that should be done first. Then, find the value of the equation.

3. $8 - 5 + 2 =$ __________ $12 \div (4 + 2) =$ __________

4. $10 - 4 \div 2 =$ __________ $[10 \div (5 - 3)] + 6 =$ __________

Name the property that each equation illustrates. The properties are commutative, associative, identity, or zero.

5. $8 + 9 = 9 + 8$ __________ $0 \div n = 0$ __________

6. $b + 0 = b$ __________ $5 \times (4 \times 7) = (5 \times 4) \times 7$ __________

Rewrite each expression using the distributive property.

7. $8 \times (3 + 6)$ __________ $(n \times 5) - (n \times 2)$ __________

8. $6a + 6b$ __________ $(f - 4) \times 7$ __________

NAME ____________________

Check What You Know

Algebra

Find the value of the variable in each equation.

	a	b	c
9.	$11 - n = 6$ ________	$t + 35 = 45$ ________	$9 \times y = 45$ ________
10.	$m \div 4 = 21$ ________	$68 = z - 13$ ________	$75 \div f = 25$ ________
11.	$p + 42 = 64$ ________	$\frac{16}{r} = 4$ ________	$\frac{n}{4} = 12$ ________

Write an equation for the problem. Then, find the value of the variable.

12. Marcos stocks shelves at a grocery. Today, he unpacked 6 boxes full of canned corn. He placed 72 cans of corn on the shelves. How many cans did each box hold?

____________________ Each box held ______ cans of corn.

Use the graph to answer the following questions.

13. How many students were enrolled in 2006?

____

14. How many more students were enrolled in 2009 than in 2006?

____

15. In which 2 years was enrollment the same?

____

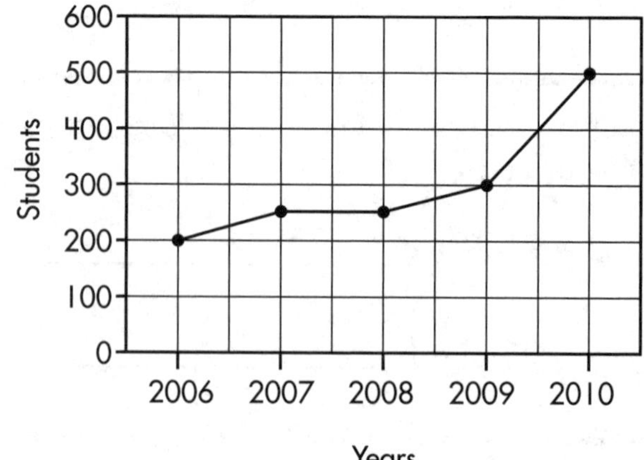

16. Enrollment increased the most between which 2 years? ____________________

How can you tell from the graph line? ____________________

NAME ____________________

Lesson 2.1 Variables, Equations, and Inequalities

An **equation** is a number sentence that contains an equals sign. An **expression** is a number phrase without an equals sign. An **inequality** shows how 2 numbers or phrases compare to one another. The inequality "2 < 4" means "2 is less than 4." The inequality "5 > 3" means "5 is greater than 3."

Equations, expressions, and inequalities may contain numerals, variables, or both. A **variable** is a symbol, usually a letter, that stands for an unknown number. A **coefficient** is a number that multiplies a variable. In the variable equation below, 2 is the coefficient of the variable *n*. In the variable expression $a - 5$, the coefficient of *a* is 1.

	Equation	*Expression*	*Inequality*
Numerical	$3 \times 5 = 15$	$9 + 2$	$17 < 20$
Variable	$2n + 4 = 18$	$a - 5$	$12 > 3d$

Identify each of the following as an equation, expression, or inequality.

	a	b	c
1.	$7 + 5$ ________	$6 + 5 = 11$ ________	$5 > 4$ ________
2.	$a + 1 < 9$ ________	$x - 5$ ________	$25 = 5b + 5$ ________

For each term below, identify the coefficient and the variable.

	a	b
3.	$8n$	y
	coefficient___ variable___	coefficient___ variable___
4.	$2x + 1$	$4 - 10d$
	coefficient___ variable___	coefficient___ variable___

Write each item as an expression, equation, or inequality. Use *n* for an unknown number.

5. 5 decreased by a number is 2 ____________________ a number is less than 4 ____________________

6. three 5s are greater than a number ____________________ two times a number, decreased by 5 ____________________

NAME ____________________

Lesson 2.2 The Order of Operations

If an expression has more than one operation, you must complete the operations in a certain order. Follow this order of operations to find the value of an expression:

1. Do operations within parentheses and brackets, innermost first.
2. Multiply and divide in order from left to right.
3. Add and subtract in order from left to right.

$4 + [12 \div (10 - 6)] \times 2 = 4 + [12 \div 4] \times 2$	Subtract (10 – 6).
$= 4 + 3 \times 2$	Divide [12 ÷ 4].
$= 4 + 6$	Multiply 3 × 2.
$= 10$	Add 4 + 6.

Underline the operation that should be done first. Then, find the value of the equation.

	a	b
1.	$12 + 9 - 14 =$ ______	$7 \times 6 \div 3 =$ ______
2.	$8 - 3 \times 2 =$ ______	$12 \div 4 + 2 =$ ______
3.	$7 \times 3 - 14 \div 2 =$ ______	$3 \times (5 + 4) =$ ______
4.	$80 \div 10 + 8 + 2 =$ ______	$80 \div (10 + 8 + 2) =$ ______
5.	$9 - 4 \times 2 \div 5 =$ ______	$(9 - 4) \times 2 \div 5 =$ ______
6.	$15 \div 5 + 7 \times 3 =$ ______	$[15 \div (5 + 7)] \times 3 =$ ______
7.	$(12 - 6) \times 2 + 15 =$ ______	$(12 - 6) \times (2 + 15) =$ ______

NAME ______________________________

Lesson 2.3 Number Properties

Commutative Property: The order in which you add numbers does not change the sum. The order in which you multiply numbers does not change the product.

$$a + b = b + a$$

$$a \times b = b \times a$$

Associative Property: The way you group addends does not change the sum. The way you group factors does not change the product.

$$a + (b + c) = (a + b) + c$$

$$a \times (b \times c) = (a \times b) \times c$$

Identity Property: The sum of an addend and 0 is the addend. The product of a factor and 1 is the factor.

$$a + 0 = a \qquad a \times 1 = a$$

Properties of Zero: The product of a factor and 0 is 0. The quotient of the dividend 0 and any divisor is 0.

$$a \times 0 = 0 \qquad 0 \div a = 0$$

Name the property that each equation illustrates.

	a	b
1.	$7 \times n = n \times 7$ ______________	$z \times 1 = z$ ______________
2.	$(w + x) + y = w + (x + y)$ ______________	$29 + 0 = 29$ ______________
3.	$47 \times 0 = 0$ ______________	$2 \times 3 \times 4 = 2 \times 4 \times 3$ ______________

Rewrite each expression using the property indicated.

4. identity: $1 \times 16 =$ ______________ associative: $(7 + t) + 8 =$ ______________

5. zero: $0 \div 14c =$ ______________ commutative: $p \times 5r =$ ______________

6. associative: $3x + (y + z) =$ ______________ identity: $90x + 0 =$ ______________

7. zero: $(w + x + y) \times 0 =$ ______________ associative: $(3xy \times 6y) \times 9 =$ ______________

NAME ______________________________

Lesson 2.4 The Distributive Property

The **Distributive Property** combines multiplication with addition and subtraction. This property states that:

$a \times (b + c) = (a \times b) + (a \times c)$	$3 \times (6 + 4) = (3 \times 6) + (3 \times 4)$
$a \times (b - c) = (a \times b) - (a \times c)$	$3 \times (10) = (18) + (12)$
	$30 = 30$

Rewrite each expression using the distributive property.

	a	b
1.	$5 \times (4 - 2) =$ ______________	$t \times (r + s) =$ ______________
2.	$(7 \times 8) + (7 \times 9) =$ ______________	$(6 - 4) \times 11 =$ ______________
3.	$5n + 5m =$ ______________	$y \times (8 - 3 - n) =$ ______________
4.	$(f + g + h) \times z =$ ______________	$(t \times t) - (t \times c) =$ ______________

Write each missing number.

5.	$(6 \times 4) + (n \times 3) = 6 \times (4 + 3)$ ________	$n \times (8 - 5) = (3 \times 8) - (3 \times 5)$ ________
6.	$(13 - n) \times 9 = (13 \times 9) - (15 \times 9)$ ________	$(3 \times 7) + (3 \times 2) = 3 \times (7 + n)$ ________
7.	$7n + 6n = 8 \times (7 + 6)$ ________	$(n \times 5) - (n \times 4) = 5 \times (5 - 4)$ ________

NAME ________________

Lesson 2.5 Solving Addition and Subtraction Equations

Addition Property of Equality: When you add the same number to both sides of an equation, the two sides remain equal.

$a = b$ $\quad a + c = b + c$

$4 + 2 = 6$ $\quad 4 + 2 + 3 = 6 + 3$ $\quad [9 = 9]$

Subtraction Property of Equality: When you subtract the same number from both sides of an equation, the two sides remain equal.

$a = b$ $\quad a - c = b - c$

$5 = 4 + 1$ $\quad 5 - 2 = 4 + 1 - 2$ $[3 = 3]$

Use these properties to find the value of variables.

$$a - 11 = 6$$
$$a - 11 + 11 = 6 + 11$$
$$a = 17$$

$$b + 3 = 14$$
$$b + 3 - 3 = 14 - 3$$
$$b = 11$$

Find the value of the variable in each equation.

	a	b	c
1.	$5 + n = 18$ ______	$16 - y = 12$ ______	$h - 9 = 9$ ______
2.	$35 + t = 35$ ______	$13 = c - 2$ ______	$17 + n = 34$ ______
3.	$m + 13 = 29$ ______	$27 + r = 51$ ______	$z - 32 = 68$ ______

Write an equation for each problem. Then, find the value of the variable.

4. Jerome made 30 cookies for the class bake sale. At the end of the sale, he had 7 cookies left. How many cookies did Jerome sell?

______________________ Jerome sold ______ cookies.

5. Grant wants to buy a bicycle that costs $219.99. He has saved $108.50 from his part–time job. How much more must Grant save to buy the bicycle?

______________________ Grant must save ______ more to buy the bicycle.

NAME ____________________

Lesson 2.6 Solving Multiplication and Division Equations

Division Property of Equality: When you divide each side of an equation by the same number, the two sides remain equal.

$a = b$
$a \div c = b \div c$
$\frac{a}{c} = \frac{b}{c}$

Multiplication Property of Equality: When you multiply each side of an equation by the same number, the two sides remain equal.

$a = b$
$a \times c = b \times c$

Use these properties to find the value of variables:

$n \div 5 = 4$
$n \div 5 \times 5 = 4 \times 5$
$n = 20$

$3 \times n = 15$
$\frac{3 \times n}{3} = \frac{15}{3}$
$n = 5$

$60 \div n = 4$
$\frac{60n}{n} = 4n$ or $60 = 4n$
$\frac{60}{4} = \frac{4n}{4}$ $15 = n$

Find the value of the variable in each equation.

	a	b	c
1.	$5 \times s = 25$ ________	$n \times 9 = 36$ ________	$a \div 7 = 8$ ________
2.	$24 \div p = 6$ ________	$154 = c \times 14 =$ ________	$\frac{r}{9} = 3$ ________
3.	$3z = 75$ ________	$16 = \frac{y}{5}$ ________	$\frac{30}{f} = 10$ ________

Write an equation for each problem. Then, find the value of the variable.

4. The tennis coach wants to buy 27 tennis balls for the team. Each can holds 3 balls. How many cans of tennis balls must the coach buy?

    ____________ The coach must buy ______ cans of tennis balls.

5. Ace Shipping Company has 168 books to ship to different bookstores. Each store will receive 12 books. How many bookstores will receive books?

    ____________ ______ bookstores will receive books.

NAME ____________________

Lesson 2.7 Reading a Graph

A graph is a way to display data visually. For example, the table lists the average temperature in Chicago, Illinois, for each month. In the line graph, you can see how average temperature rises and falls from month to month.

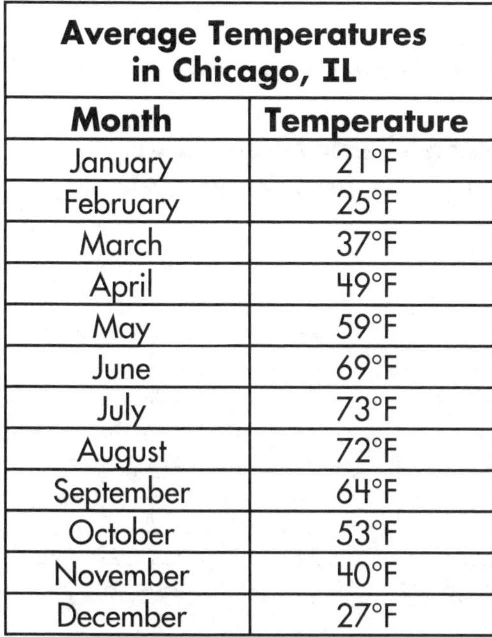

Average Temperatures in Chicago, IL	
Month	**Temperature**
January	21°F
February	25°F
March	37°F
April	49°F
May	59°F
June	69°F
July	73°F
August	72°F
September	64°F
October	53°F
November	40°F
December	27°F

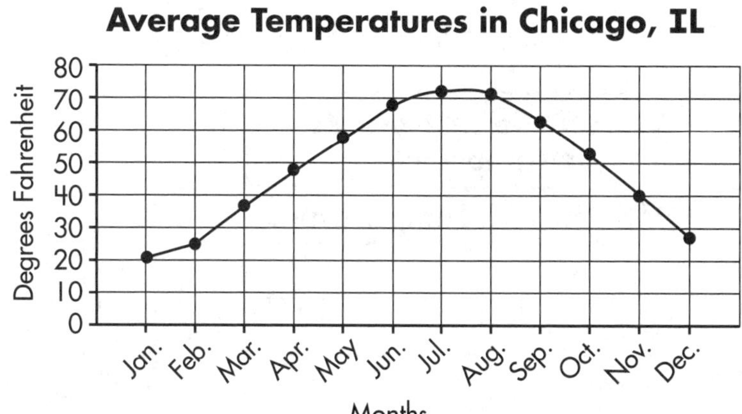

In the graph above, the values along the horizontal axis, or *x*–axis, are months. The values along the vertical axis, or *y*–axis, are degrees Fahrenheit (°F).

Each row in the table gives a pair of values: a month and a temperature for that month. Each pair represents a point on the graph. To find the values of a point on the graph, look down from the point to the month on the *x*–axis. Look across from the point to the degrees on the *y*–axis. For example, the month directly down from the first dot is January. The number of degrees across from the dot is 21. This dot represents January, 21°F.

Use the table and graph to answer these questions.

1. What is Chicago's highest average temperature? __________ lowest? __________

2. How many degrees does Chicago's average temperature rise from its lowest value to its highest? Write an equation for this problem. Then, solve it.

____________________ Chicago's average temperature rises __________ °F.

NAME ___________________________

Lesson 2.7 Reading a Graph

The graph below shows the average temperatures in two cities: Chicago (from the previous page) and Tampa, Florida.

Use the graph to answer these questions.

3. Write in the table the average temperature in Tampa, Florida, for each month.

Average Temperatures in Tampa, FL	
Month	**Temperature**
January	
February	
March	
April	
May	
June	
July	
August	
September	
October	
November	
December	

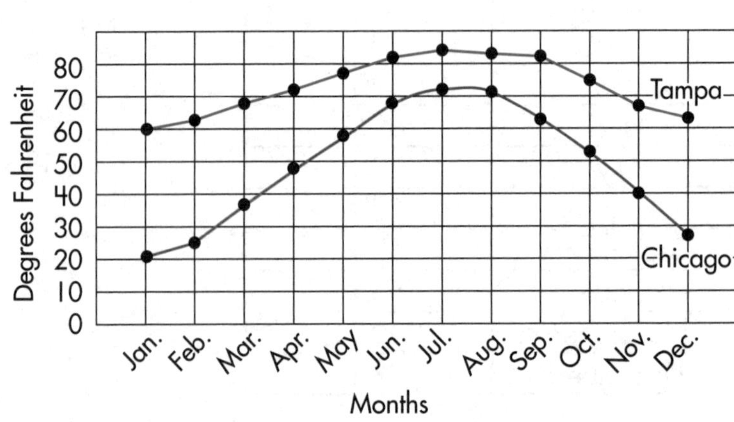

4. What is Tampa's highest average temperature? __________ lowest? __________

5. How many degrees does Tampa's average temperature rise from its lowest value to its highest? Write an equation for this problem. Then, solve it.

____________________ Tampa's average temperature rises __________ °F.

6. Which city has the greatest difference between its highest and lowest average temperature?

__________ How can you tell by comparing the two graph lines?

____

NAME ______________________

Check What You Learned

Algebra

Identify the coefficient and the variable in each term below.

	a	b
1.	$15y$	$6 + 4c$
	coefficient____ variable____	coefficient____ variable____

Write each item as an expression, equation, or inequality. Use n for an unknown number.

2. 33 increased by a number times 6 ______________________ a number decreased by 4 is less than 8 ______________________

Underline the operation that should be done first. Then, find the value of the equation.

3. $2 \times 5 \div 5 =$ ______________ $18 \div 6 + 3 =$ ______________

4. $3 \times 8 \div (2 + 10) =$ ______________ $[20 \div (10 - 5)] + 1 =$ ______________

Rewrite each expression using the property indicated.

5. zero: $0 \div 3p =$ ______________ associative: $4a \times (3b \times c)$ ______________

6. identity: $6g \times 1 =$ ______________ commutative: $9r + 17s =$ ______________

Rewrite each expression using the distributive property.

7. $9 \times (8 + m) =$ ______________ $8q - 8r =$ ______________

8. $13y + 7y =$ ______________ $(5 + 4 + 3) \times q =$ ______________

CHAPTER 2 POSTTEST

NAME ____________________

Check What You Learned

Algebra

Find the value of the variable in each equation.

	a	b	c
9.	$33 + n = 72$ ______	$p - 54 = 23$ ______	$13 \times m = 156$ ______
10.	$b \div 14 = 11$ ______	$129 \div r = 43$ ______	$205 - g = 108$ ______
11.	$54 = q + 17$ ______	$6h = 96$ ______	$\frac{300}{t} = 60$ ______

Write an equation for the problem. Then, find the value of the variable.

12. Tanya collected trash in the park as a school project. On Friday, she collected 8 pounds of trash. On Saturday, she collected 10 pounds. By the end of the weekend, she had collected 35 pounds of trash. How much trash did she collect on Sunday?

______________ Tanya collected ______ pounds on Sunday.

Use the graph to answer the following questions.

Jamal's Height

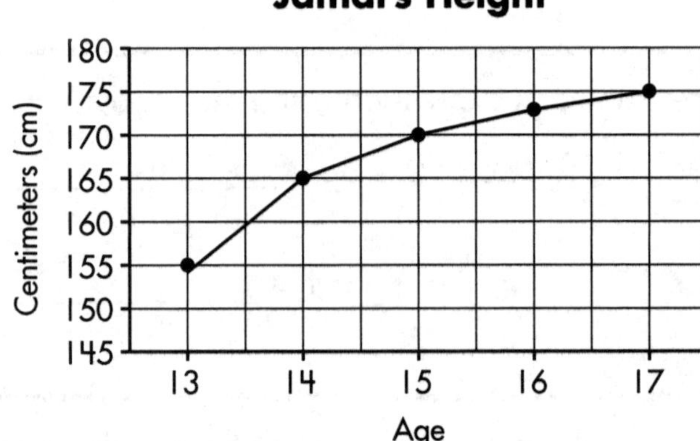

13. How tall was Jamal at age 14?

______

14. How many centimeters did Jamal grow between ages 13 and 14? ______

15. How many centimeters did Jamal grow between ages 14 and 15? ______

16. Is Jamal growing faster or slower as he gets older? ______
How can you tell from the shape of the graph line?

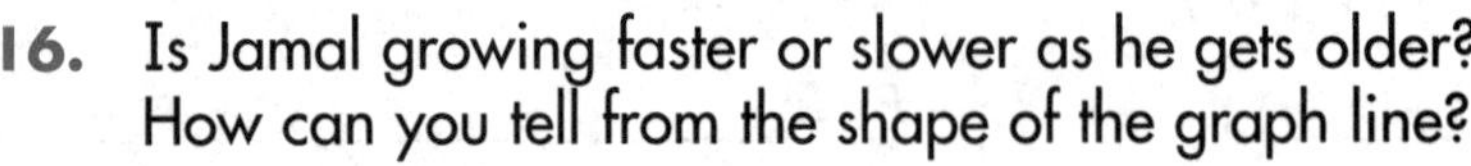

____

NAME ____________________

Check What You Know

Graphing Ratios

Find the unknown number in each proportion.

	a	b	c
1.	$\frac{1}{4} = \frac{n}{12}$ ______	$\frac{n}{20} = \frac{3}{12}$ ______	$\frac{1}{9} = \frac{n}{72}$ ______
2.	$\frac{n}{20} = \frac{8}{80}$ ______	$\frac{90}{180} = \frac{n}{54}$ ______	$\frac{4}{8} = \frac{12}{n}$ ______

Write the symbol > or < to compare each pair of numbers.

3.	–1 ______ 1	10 ______ –10	–7 ______ –8
4.	–9 ______ –6	5 ______ –5	9 ______ –4

Add, subtract, multiply, or divide.

5.	9 + (–1) = ______	–6 + (–6) = ______	–8 + 2 = ______
6.	–14 ÷ 7 = ______	–41 x (–11) = ______	90 ÷ (–2) = ______

Write an equation for each problem. Then, solve.

7. Shannon made $75 this year selling aluminum cans to the recycling center. The recycling center pays for aluminum by the pound, and Shannon had collected 300 pounds. Next year, she wants to make $120. How many pounds of cans does she need to collect next year?

________________ Shannon must collect ________ pounds of cans.

8. Maxine earns a commission on the products she sells. She earned $3,600 last year on sales of $30,000. This year she wants to make $5,400. How much does she need to sell?

________________ Maxine needs sales of $________.

NAME ____________________

Check What You Know

Graphing Ratios

The responses to a phone survey are shown in the table.

	Males				Females			
Question	**Age 18–25**		**Age 26–32**		**Age 18–25**		**Age 26–32**	
	Yes	**No**	**Yes**	**No**	**Yes**	**No**	**Yes**	**No**
1	388	212	289	311	208	392	299	301
2	122	478	302	298	132	468	322	278
3	271	329	308	292	380	220	293	307
4	220	380	340	260	244	356	296	304

9. How many males took the survey? __________ How many females? __________

10. How many people are in each age group? __________

11. What fraction of all males age 18–25 responded *no* to question 4? __________

What percent of all males age 18–25 responded *no* to question 4? __________

12. How many females age 26–32 responded *yes* to question 3? __________

What percent of all females age 26–32 responded *yes* to question 3? __________

Plot each ordered pair on Grid 1.

13. *A* (2, 3) *B* (−5, 4)

14. *C* (−5, −3) *D* (6, −8)

15. *E* (5, 3) *F* (−1, 7)

Grid 1

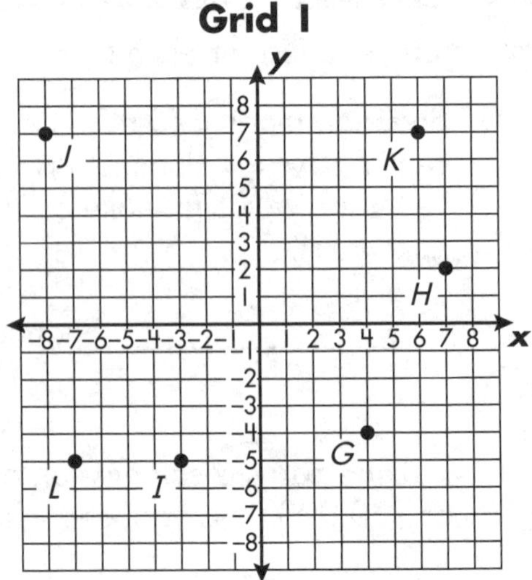

Write the ordered pair that locates each of these points on Grid 1.

16. *G* _______ *H* _______

17. *I* _______ *J* _______

18. *K* _______ *L* _______

NAME ________________________________

Lesson 3.1 Ratio and Proportion

A **ratio** compares the numbers in 2 sets. A ratio can be expressed as 1 to 2, 1:2, or $\frac{1}{2}$. In this example, the ratio means that for every 1 of the first item, there are 2 of the other item.

A **proportion** expresses the equality of 2 ratios. Cross-multiply to determine if two ratios are equal. If the ratios are equal, then they are a true proportion.

$\frac{4}{2} \times \frac{2}{1}$ $4 \times 1 = 2 \times 2$, so it is true. $\frac{3}{4} = \frac{2}{3}$ $3 \times 3 \neq 4 \times 2$, so it is not true.

Cross-multiply to check each proportion. Write *true* next to each true proportion.

	a	b	c
1.	$\frac{1}{3} = \frac{2}{6}$ ______	$\frac{5}{8} = \frac{6}{15}$ ______	1 to 8 = 2:3 ______
2.	1:2 = 5:10 ______	$\frac{1}{5}$ = 7 to 35 ______	$\frac{2}{4} = \frac{7}{28}$ ______
3.	$\frac{5}{15} = \frac{1}{3}$ ______	$\frac{4}{12} = \frac{1}{5}$ ______	$\frac{7}{14} = \frac{1}{3}$ ______
4.	$\frac{6}{24} = \frac{3}{12}$ ______	$\frac{3}{15} = \frac{6}{30}$ ______	6:18 = 3:12 ______
5.	$\frac{3}{15} = \frac{27}{135}$ ______	5:12 = 7:35 ______	$\frac{4}{12} = \frac{7}{21}$ ______
6.	$\frac{2}{8} = \frac{5}{16}$ ______	1:9 = 9:81 ______	1:5 = 2 to 10 ______
7.	$\frac{2}{6} = \frac{8}{32}$ ______	$\frac{4}{8} = \frac{10}{20}$ ______	$\frac{3}{18} = \frac{6}{60}$ ______

NAME ______________________

Lesson 3.1 Ratio and Proportion

A proportion can be used to solve problems.

In a recent election, fewer votes were cast by people under the age of 50 than by those over the age of 50 by a ratio of 5:6. There were 1,200 voters over the age of 50. How many voters were under the age of 50?

$\frac{5}{6} = \frac{n}{1{,}200}$	Write the ratio as a fraction. Set up a proportion using *n* for the missing number.
$5 \times 1{,}200 = 6 \times n$	Cross-multiply.
$\frac{6{,}000}{6} = n$	Solve for *n*.
$1{,}000 = n$	There were 1,000 voters under the age of 50.

Solve each of the following.

	a	b	c
1.	$\frac{3}{4} = \frac{n}{32}$ ________	$\frac{5}{n} = \frac{25}{50}$ ________	$\frac{n}{6} = \frac{8}{48}$ ________
2.	$\frac{1}{n} = \frac{10}{30}$ ________	$\frac{1}{2} = \frac{18}{n}$ ________	$\frac{12}{16} = \frac{n}{84}$ ________
3.	$\frac{12}{32} = \frac{n}{160}$ ________	$\frac{90}{180} = \frac{n}{10}$ ________	$\frac{16}{320} = \frac{n}{40}$ ________

Write an equation for each problem. Then, solve.

4. Oakmont collected $18,612 last year for 4,400 pounds of copper pipe it recycled from old buildings. This year, the city wants to make $20,000. How many pounds of copper will it need to recycle? Round to the nearest pound.

________________ Oakmont must recycle ________ pounds of copper.

5. Rose Coffee Company will ship 4,000 pounds of coffee from the United States to Canada next month. It has to pay a tax of $4.20 for every 100 pounds it ships. How much tax will it pay on the coffee?

________________ The company will pay a tax of ________ dollars.

NAME ______________________________

Lesson 3.2 Solving Proportion Equations

Find the unknown number in each proportion. Follow these steps.

	1. Cross-multiply to make an equation.	2. Divide both sides by the number with *n*.	3. What is *n*?
$\frac{4}{5} = \frac{n}{15}$	$4 \times 15 = 5 \times n$ $60 = 5n$	$60 \div 5 = 5n \div 5$ $12 = n$	12
$\frac{14}{7} = \frac{4}{n}$	$14 \times n = 4 \times 7$ $14n = 28$	$14n \div 14 = 28 \div 14$ $n = 2$	2
$\frac{n}{5} = \frac{4}{20}$	$n \times 20 = 4 \times 5$ $20n = 20$	$20n \div 20 = 20 \div 20$ $n = 1$	1
$\frac{6}{n} = \frac{9}{3}$	$6 \times 3 = 9 \times n$ $18 = 9n$	$18 \div 9 = 9n \div 9$ $2 = n$	2

Solve for *n* in each proportion.

	a	b	c
1.	$\frac{1}{3} = \frac{n}{9}$ ________	$\frac{12}{8} = \frac{n}{64}$ ________	$\frac{1}{n} = \frac{5}{10}$ ________
2.	$\frac{12}{n} = \frac{24}{64}$ ________	$\frac{1}{9} = \frac{n}{81}$ ________	$\frac{n}{4} = \frac{7}{28}$ ________
3.	$\frac{4}{32} = \frac{10}{n}$ ________	$\frac{4}{20} = \frac{n}{5}$ ________	$\frac{9}{n} = \frac{81}{99}$ ________

Write an equation for each problem. Then, solve.

4. After a trip, Michael calculated that he traveled 400 miles on 20 gallons of gas. He drove 220 miles from his starting point to Taylorsville. How many gallons of gas did he use to get to Taylorsville?

____________ Michael used ______ gallons of gas.

5. Carol is preparing flower arrangements with 2 red roses for every 6 yellow roses. She has 48 yellow roses. How many red roses does she need?

____________ Carol needs ______ red roses.

NAME ____________________

Lesson 3.2 Solving Proportion Equations

Use proportions to solve each problem. Show your work.

1. A group is doing a 7–day walk covering 150 miles for charity. During the first 4 days, the leader recorded the data in the table. The group is trying to walk 7–8 hours per day to finish on time. The table shows the group was delayed by rain on days 2 and 4. No rain is expected on days 5–7, so the group should be able to walk 8 hours on each of those days.

	Hours Walked	**Miles Walked**
Day 1	8	24
Day 2	6.5	19.5
Day 3	9	27
Day 4	4	12
Totals	27.5	82.5

a. How many miles per hour does the group walk? ____________

b. How many miles are left to walk? ____________

c. Do you predict that the group will finish the walk on day 7? Explain.

____

2. A college football stadium has 20,400 seats. The school will set aside 1 out of every 50 seats for its students. How many seats will be set aside for students?

________ seats will be set aside for students.

3. Wilson practices basketball 3 hours per day every day of the week. For every hour he practices, he studies 15 minutes. How much time does he study each week?

Wilson studies _______ hours each week.

4. For her business, Carla drove from Billings, Montana, to Boise, Idaho—a distance of 600 miles. The drive took 8 hours. If she drives at the same speed, how long will it take her to reach her next stop 450 miles away?

Carla will reach her next stop in _______ hours.

NAME ___________________________

Lesson 3.3 Interpreting Data Using Ratios and Percents

You can use ratios and percentages to analyze information. For example, a phone survey collected the data in the table below.

How many people participated in the sample?

1,200 (Total the number of people who responded to any one question.)

How many males and females responded? *Males: 380 Females: 820*

What is the overall ratio of males to females in the sample? *380:820 or 19:41*

What percent of the total respondents are male? female?

Male: 380 ÷ 1,200 = 32% *Female: 820 ÷ 1,200 = 68%* (rounded)

What percent of males and females responded *yes* to question 5?

Males: 82% *Females: 10%* (rounded)

	Male		**Female**	
Question	**Yes**	**No**	**Yes**	**No**
1	60	320	412	408
2	45	335	320	500
3	175	205	578	242
4	280	100	644	176
5	310	70	82	738

Solve each problem. Refer to the table at right. Show your work.

1. Students at Lincoln High School sold cookies for three weeks last spring. They sold three kinds of cookies, as shown in the table. Write a ratio that compares the total boxes of chocolate cookies sold to the total of all boxes sold. What percentage of all boxes sold were chocolate? Round to the nearest whole percent.

Lincoln High Cookie Sales			
	Week 1	**Week 2**	**Week 3**
Shortbread	65	120	180
Chocolate	84	151	380
Lemon	23	85	97

_______________ Of all boxes sold, ________ percent were chocolate.

2. Next spring, students will sell a fourth flavor of cookie, coconut. Based on sales at another school, they expect to sell about 4 boxes of coconut cookies for every 5 boxes of shortbread cookies. About how many boxes of coconut cookies can they expect to sell? Write a proportion equation to find the answer.

_______________ Students can expect to sell ______ boxes.

NAME ______________________

Lesson 3.3 Interpreting Data Using Ratios and Percents

Solve each problem. Show your work.

1. For every pound of Gala apples he bought, Paul purchased 3 pounds of Winesap apples. He bought 5 pounds of Gala apples at $6.46 per pound. The Winesaps cost the same as the Gala. How much did he pay for the Winesap apples?

Paul paid $________ for the Winesap apples.

2. The superintendent needs to know the ratio of boys to girls in two local schools. He has the data in the tables at right. What is the ratio of boys to girls in each school? Reduce the ratios to their simplest form.

Wilson Middle School Enrollment

Grade	Boys	Girls
6	222	161
7	276	240
8	252	199

Wilson High School Enrollment

Grade	Boys	Girls
9	492	470
10	321	502
11	430	488
12	257	415

Ratio of boys to girls in:

middle school __________ high school __________

3. Lisa works an 8-hour day. She has earned 5.5 days vacation time after working for the company for 7 months. She wants to take a long trip after she has worked for 1 year. How many hours of vacation time will she have then? Round your answer to the nearest full hour.

Lisa will have _______ hours of vacation time.

4. In a poll of 1,500 voters, 1,200 approved of the mayor's performance. The mayor told the newspaper that 90% approved of his work. Was the mayor correct?

______________ percent of voters approve. Was the mayor correct? _______

5. A basketball player scored about 22 points per game his first year. The season is 30 games long. At this rate, does he have a good chance of breaking the team record of 2,940 points before his college career ends in 3 years?

At this rate, the player will score ______________ total points.

At this rate, will the player break the record? ________

NAME ______________________

Lesson 3.4 Comparing and Ordering Integers

Integers are the set of whole numbers and their opposites. You need to understand integers to create graphs on a coordinate plane.

Positive integers are greater than zero. **Negative integers** are less than zero. Zero is neither positive nor negative. A negative integer is less than a positive integer. On a number line, an integer and its opposite are the same distance from zero. The smaller of two integers is always the one to the left on a number line.

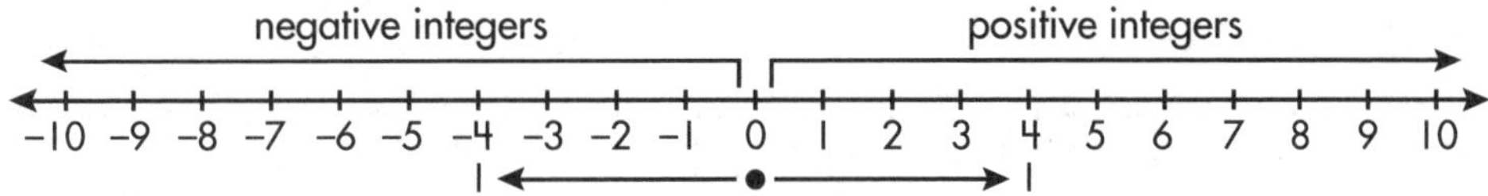

The opposite of 4 is −4. They are both 4 spaces from 0.

−7 < −2 −7 is to the left of −2. −4 > −9 −4 is to the right of −9.

Use integers to name each point on the number line.

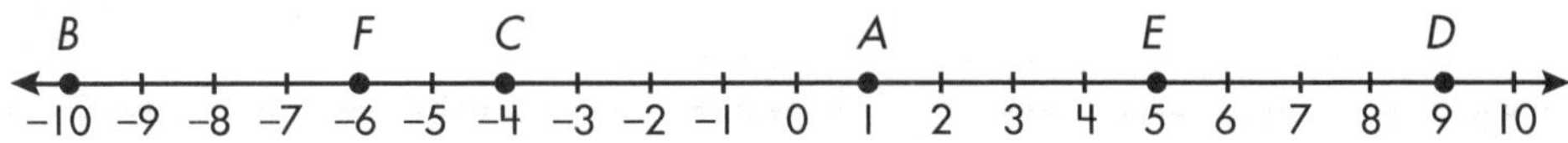

	a	b	c
1.	D ________	A ________	B ________
2.	E ________	C ________	F ________

Write the symbol > or < to compare each pair of numbers.

3.	4 ______ 9	−4 ______ −3	−1 ______ −2
4.	−2 ______ 2	6 ______ −8	−7 ______ −8

Order column A from smallest to largest. Order column B from largest to smallest.

	a	b
5.	−3, −10, 0 ____________	9, −1, 4 ____________
6.	−10, −8, −3 ____________	−5, −8, −2 ____________

NAME ______________________

Lesson 3.5 Adding and Subtracting Integers

The sum of two positive integers is positive. The sum of two negative integers is negative.

$4 + 3 = 7$

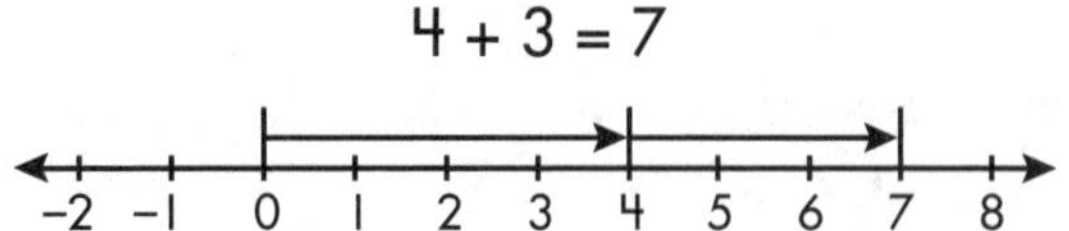

$-4 + (-3) = -7$

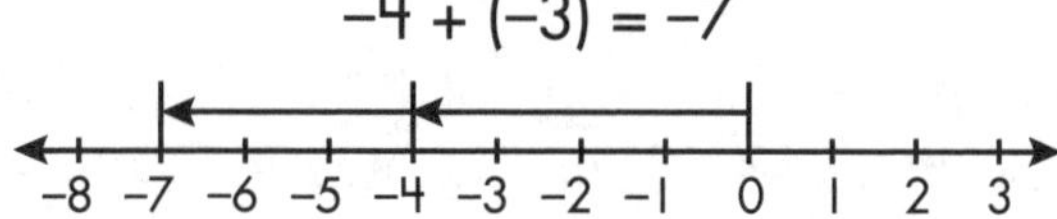

To find the sum of two integers with different signs, find their absolute values. **Absolute value** is the distance (in units) that a number is from 0 expressed as a positive quantity. Subtract the lesser number from the greater number. Absolute value is written as $|x|$.

$-4 + 3 = -1$

$|-4| = 4 \quad 4 - 3 = 1$

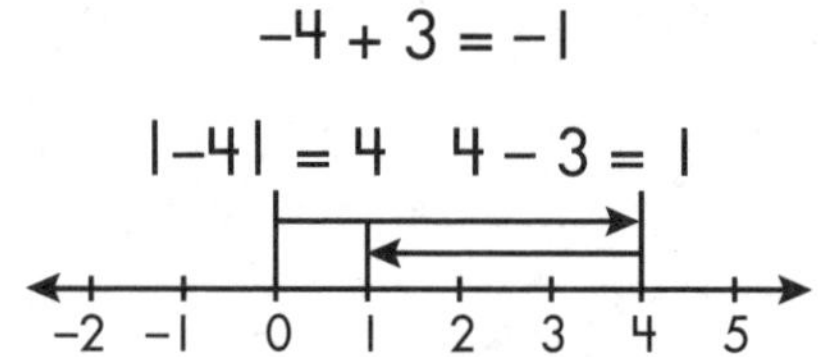

The sum has the same sign as the integer with the larger absolute value.

$4 > 3$, so the sum is negative.

To subtract an integer, add its opposite.

$5 - 7 = 5 + (-7) = -2$

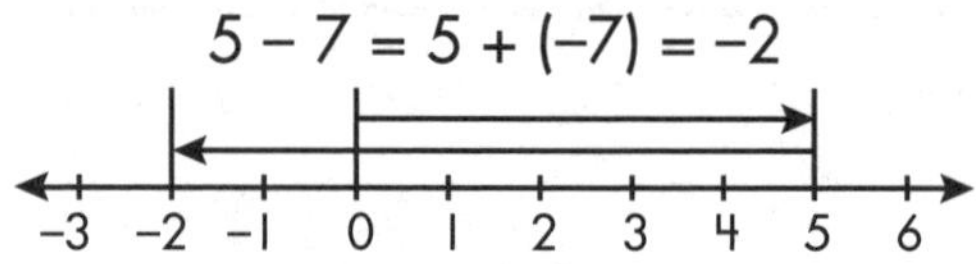

Add or subtract.

	a	b	c
1.	$8 + 3 =$ ______	$-2 + 3 =$ ______	$-4 + (-5) =$ ______
2.	$-8 + 5 =$ ______	$-12 - (-3) =$ ______	$-5 + 5 =$ ______
3.	$8 + 6 =$ ______	$-9 - (-1) =$ ______	$-11 - (-5) =$ ______
4.	$0 + (-6) =$ ______	$-1 + (-3) =$ ______	$-9 - (-8) =$ ______
5.	$10 + (-2) =$ ______	$2 - (-1) =$ ______	$4 + (-9) =$ ______
6.	$-9 + (-2) =$ ______	$12 - (-1) =$ ______	$4 + (-4) =$ ______

NAME ______________________

Lesson 3.6 Multiplying and Dividing Integers

The product of two integers with the same sign is positive.	$3 \times 3 = 9$ $-3 \times -3 = 9$
The product of two integers with different signs is negative.	$3 \times (-3) = -9$ $-3 \times 3 = -9$
The quotient of two integers with the same sign is positive.	$8 \div 2 = 4$ $-8 \div (-2) = 4$
The quotient of two integers with different signs is negative.	$8 \div (-2) = -4$ $-8 \div 2 = -4$

Multiply or divide.

	a	b	c
1.	$4 \times 9 =$ ______	$-24 \div 3 =$ ______	$-16 \div 8 =$ ______
2.	$-2 \times 2 =$ ______	$-6 \div (-2) =$ ______	$-14 \times 7 =$ ______
3.	$60 \div (-10) =$ ______	$-5 \times -6 =$ ______	$-22 \div 2 =$ ______
4.	$-1 \times 4 =$ ______	$48 \div 8 =$ ______	$-10 \times (-7) =$ ______
5.	$14 \times (-14) =$ ______	$78 \div (-6) =$ ______	$2 \times 12 =$ ______
6.	$70 \div (-5) =$ ______	$-98 \times (-2) =$ ______	$-32 \div (-8) =$ ______
7.	$100 \div 5 =$ ______	$40 \times (-6) =$ ______	$14 \div (-7) =$ ______

NAME ______________________

Lesson 3.7 Plotting Ordered Pairs

Two intersecting number lines form a coordinate plane. The **x-axis** is the horizontal line. The **y-axis** is the vertical line.

An ordered pair of numbers locates the position of any point on a coordinate plane. The numbers in an ordered pair are expressed in this order: (x, y). Each number in the pair shows the distance the point is from the origin (0, 0). The first number shows distance from the origin along the *x*-axis. The second number shows the distance from the origin along the *y*-axis. In the graph at right, point *A* is located at (4, 2). Point *B* is located at (–5, –3).

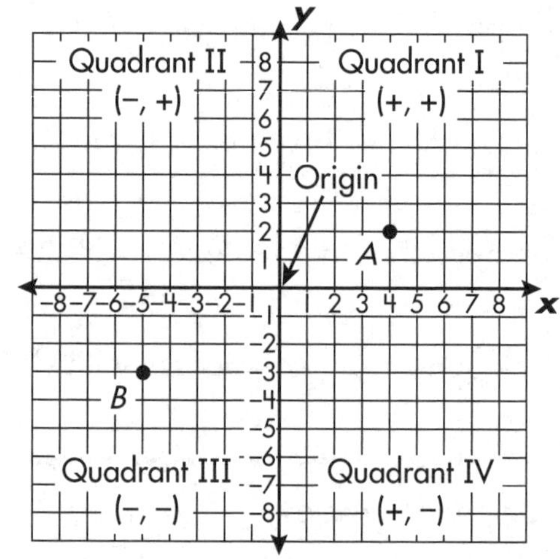

Plot each ordered pair on Grid 1.

1. *A* (1, 2) *B* (–5, 2)

2. *C* (–7, –2) *D* (8, –8)

3. *E* (6, 4) *F* (–2, 3)

4. *G* (–6, –4) *H* (8, –7)

5. *I* (8, 5) *J* (2, –3)

Grid 1

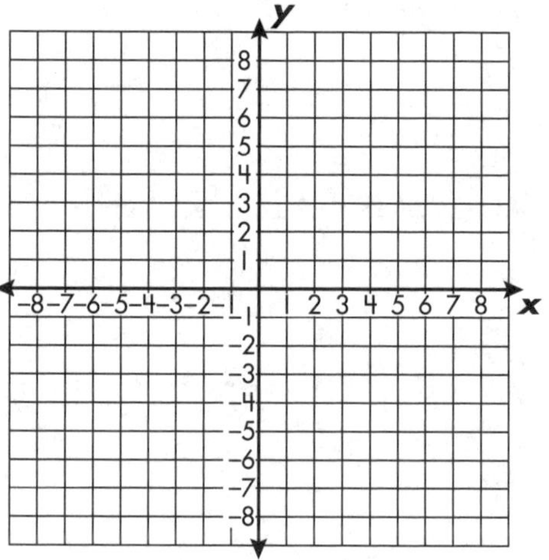

Write the ordered pair that locates each lettered point on Grid 2.

6. *A* __________ *B* __________

7. *C* __________ *D* __________

8. *E* __________ *F* __________

9. *G* __________ *H* __________

10. *I* __________ *J* __________

Grid 2

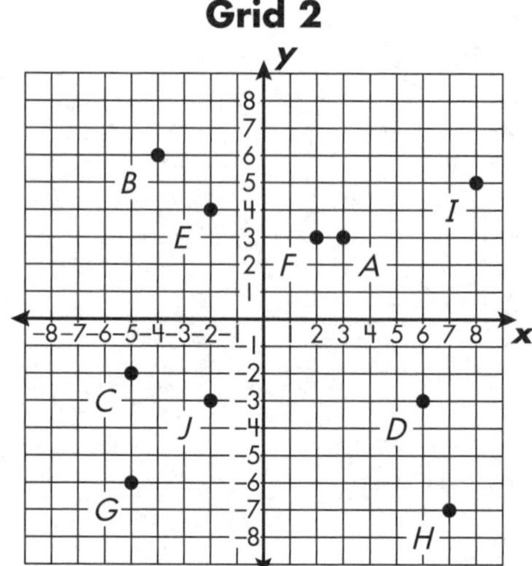

NAME ____________________

Lesson 3.7 Plotting Ordered Pairs

Plot each ordered pair on Grid 1.

Grid 1

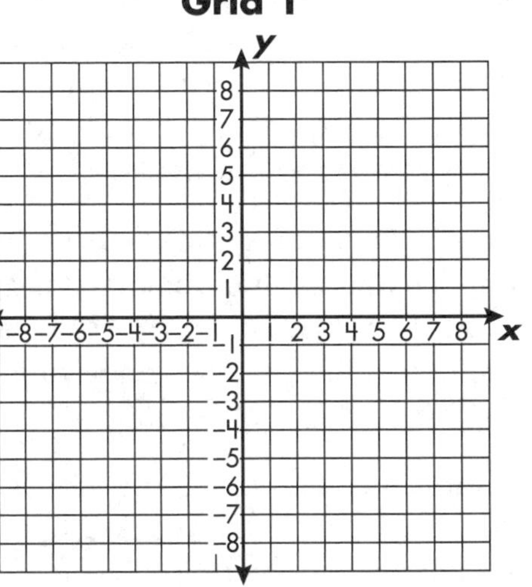

1. A (−3, −3) B (−2, 4)

2. C (7, 5) D (−8, 7)

3. E (5, 5) F (2, −3)

4. G (−2, −8) H (4, −6)

5. I (2, 2) J (−6, 2)

6. During an archaeological dig, scientists kept track of where artifacts (bits of pottery) were found. The center of the dig is located at the origin (0,0) of Grid 2. Each square in the grid represents 10 feet from the origin. In Grid 2, the *y*-axis points north and south. The *x*-axis points east and west. The table identifies the locations of artifacts by the direction and number of feet from the origin. In the table, convert the locations to (*x*, *y*) coordinates. Plot the location of the artifacts on the grid.

a. Which quadrant had the most artifacts? __________

b. Which two quadrants had the same number of artifacts? __________

Artifact	Location (feet)	(x, y) Coordinates
A	50W, 40N	
B	20E, 20N	
C	80W, 70S	
D	40E, 70N	
E	20E, 40N	
F	60W, 50S	
G	70E, 40S	
H	40W, 30S	
I	70W, 60N	
J	70E, 40N	
K	30E, 20S	
L	40W, 50N	

Grid 2

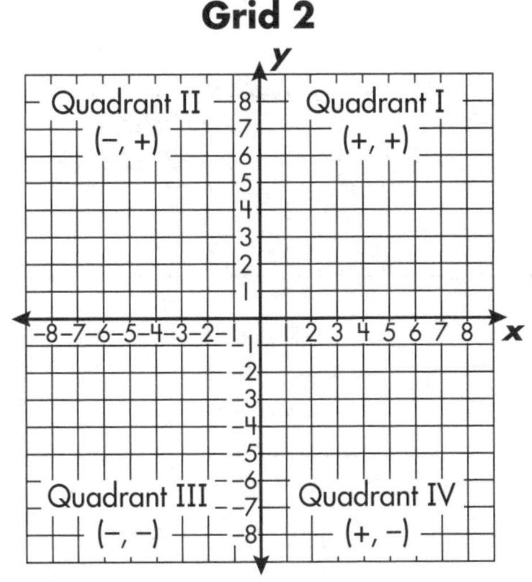

NAME ______________________

Lesson 3.8 Graphing Ratios

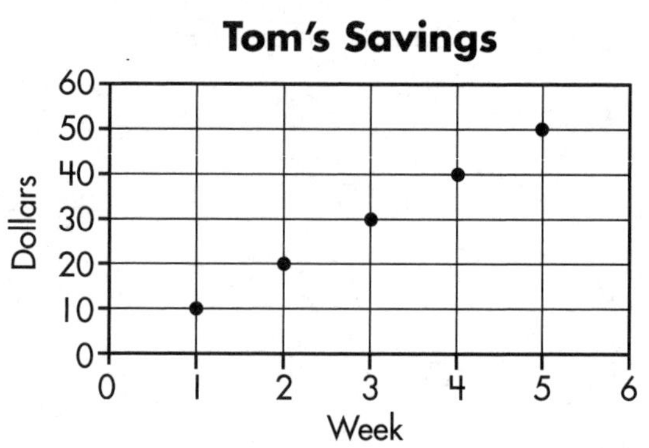

Any set of ordered pairs is a **relation**, because each pair relates two values. Think of the graph at right as Quadrant I of a coordinate plane. Tom deposits $10 into his savings account each week. The graph relates Tom's savings to the week.

The **domain** of a relation is all the *x*-values in the set. In this example, the domain is the set of values {1, 2, 3, 4, 5}. The **range** of a relation is all the *y*-values in the set. The range of this relation is {$10, $20, $30, $40, $50}.

What is the ratio of dollars to weeks in Week 5? *5 weeks to $50, or 1:10.* Is the ratio for Week 3 the same? *Yes. 3:30 = 1:10.* Draw a line connecting the points. Note that the line is a straight line. Only relations with a constant (unchanging) ratio form a straight line on a graph. A relation with changing ratios form a curved line.

Week (*x*-values)	**Dollars (*y*-values)**
1	10
2	20
3	30
4	40
5	50

Solve this problem.

1. For her business, Carey's Roses, Carey buys a box of two dozen roses wholesale for $20. Make a table and graph of her costs for 2, 4, 6, and 8 boxes of roses. Be sure to label the *x*-axis and *y*-axis in your graph.

What would Carey's cost be for 20 dozen roses? ________

Boxes (*x* values)	**Dollars (*y* values)**

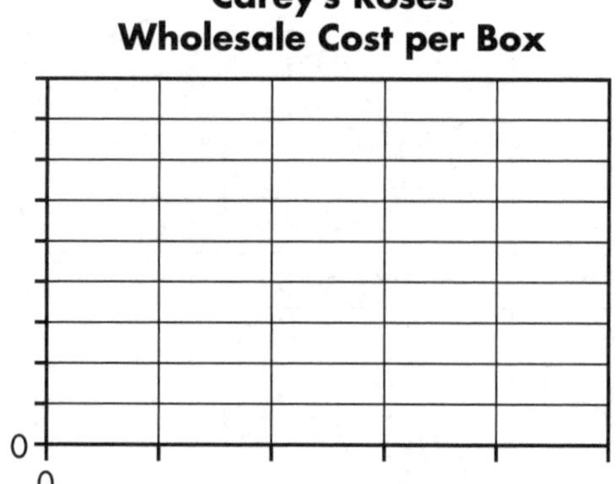

NAME ____________________

Lesson 3.8 Graphing Ratios

1. Bob and Jack went on a trip together driving separate cars. The table gives data from the 5 legs of their trip. They followed the same route at the same speed. Graph the 5 legs of their trip on the grid below. For each leg in the trip, mark a dot on the graph for Bob's gas use and an *x* on the graph for Jack's gas use.

   Based on the graph, how did Jack's use of gas compare to Bob's?

   ____

Leg	Distance Traveled (miles)	Bob's Gas Use (gallons)	Jack's Gas Use (gallons)
1	190	7	6.5
2	228	7.5	7
3	260	9	8.5
4	282	11.5	9.5
5	325	12.5	11.5

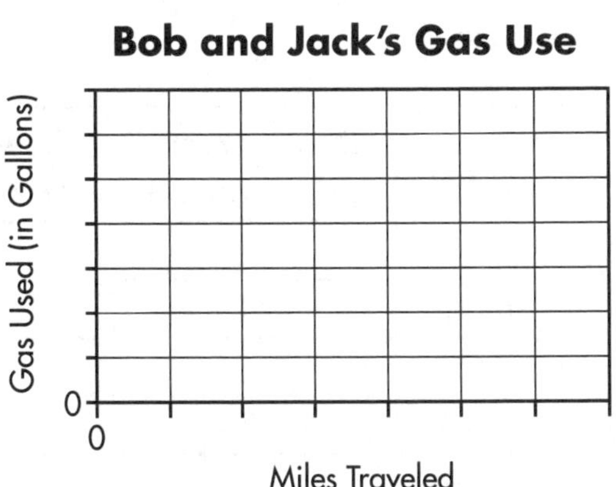

2. Ms. Rivera recorded her students' average study hours per week and course grade, as shown in the table. Make a graph of the data. Label the *x*- and *y*-axes.

   Based on your graph, how are number of study hours related to grade?

   ____

Student	Study Hours per Week	Course Grade
Sheree	5	98
Paul	1.5	60
Tom	4	90
Marcus	4.5	93
Linda	2	70
Alicia	3	84
Pat	2	65

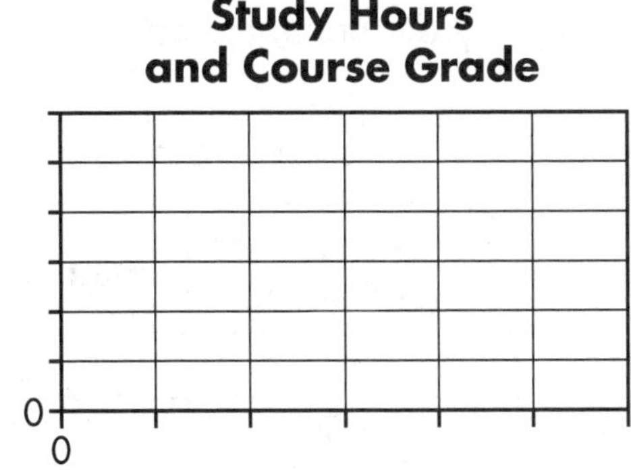

NAME ______________________________

Lesson 3.9 Problem Solving

Solve each problem.

1. During a science experiment, Martin recorded the data in the table over a period of one month. Graph the data. Make sure to label the *x*-axis and *y*-axis.

Describe the relationship between daily hours of sunlight and weekly plant growth.

____

Circle the points that show where additional hours of sunlight no longer increase plant growth.

Plant	Daily Hours of Sunlight	Weekly Plant Growth (cm)
A	2	1.25
B	4	2.75
C	6	4
D	8	5.25
E	10	5.5
F	12	5.5

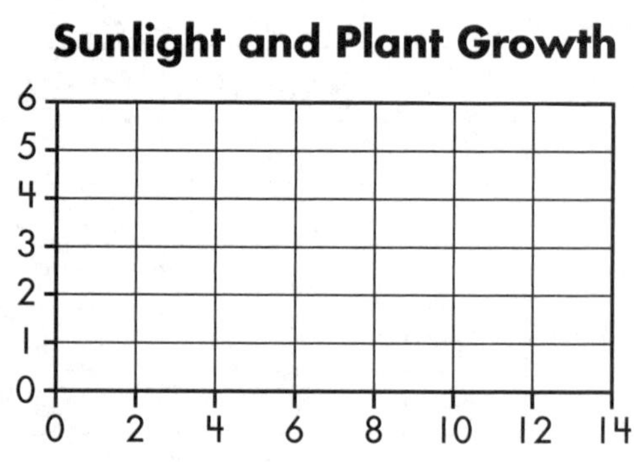

2. Sandy recorded the data in the table below during his vacation. Graph the data.

a. Describe the relationship between the hours Sandy fished and the fish he caught.

____

b. What day did not fit the pattern in the graph?

____

Day	Fishing Hours per Day	Fish Caught
Mon	5	8
Tues	4.5	2
Wed	3	3
Thurs	7.25	13
Fri	8	14
Sat	6.5	12
Sun	4.5	7

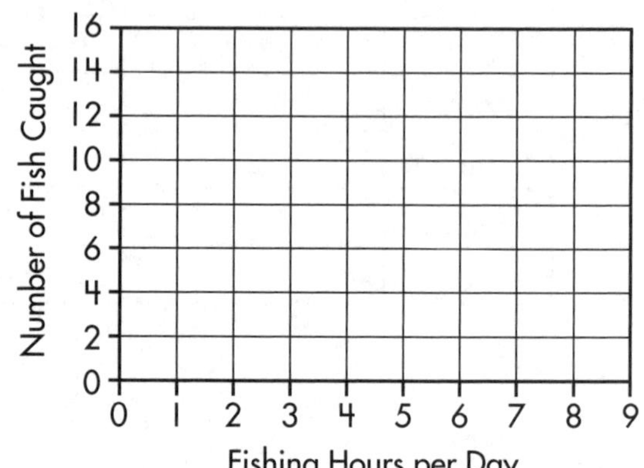

NAME ____________________

Check What You Learned

Graphing Ratios

Find the unknown number in each proportion.

	a	b	c
1.	$\frac{3}{3} = \frac{n}{9}$ ______	$\frac{6}{42} = \frac{10}{n}$ ______	$\frac{5}{n} = \frac{2}{4}$ ______
2.	$\frac{n}{12} = \frac{1}{6}$ ______	$\frac{9}{n} = \frac{3}{6}$ ______	$\frac{2}{14} = \frac{4}{n}$ ______
3.	$\frac{n}{10} = \frac{6}{60}$ ______	$\frac{1}{n} = \frac{2}{16}$ ______	$\frac{8}{40} = \frac{1}{n}$ ______

Add, subtract, multiply, or divide.

4.	$3 + (-5) =$ ______	$-2 + (-9) =$ ______	$-7 \times (-5) =$ ______
5.	$-4 - (-2) =$ ______	$-5 + 12 =$ ______	$-9 \div (-3) =$ ______
6.	$81 \times (-5) =$ ______	$-99 \times 1 =$ ______	$66 \div (-11) =$ ______

Write a proportion equation to solve each problem. Show your work.

7. A manufacturer found 25 defective computers out of 4,500 it made. In a batch of 27,000 computers, how many defective ones can the company expect to find?

   The company can expect to find ______ defective computers.

8. For every $1,000 he earns, Wilson puts $80 in his savings account. This year he will earn $15,000. How much will he save?

   ____________ Wilson will save $________.

CHAPTER 3 POSTTEST

NAME ____________________

Check What You Learned

Graphing Ratios

Label each quadrant of Grid 1 (Q1 has been labeled for you). Then, plot each ordered pair on Grid 1.

9. *A* (3, −2) *B* (2, 5)

10. *C* (8, 4) *D* (−4, 2)

11. *E* (4, 3) *F* (−2, −3)

12. *G* (−4, −3) *H* (4, −4)

13. *I* (−6, 3) *J* (−7, −8)

Grid 1

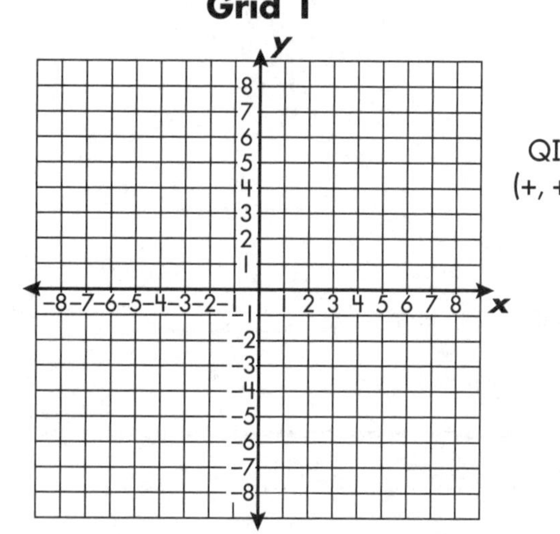

CHAPTER 3 POSTTEST

Complete the table and graph.

14. Peggy goes to the grocery every day. Monday through Wednesday, she gets a 10% discount on the amount she spends. Thursday through Sunday she gets a 5% discount. Calculate the missing data in the table. Plot the data on the graph. Circle the data points on the graph where Peggy saved the largest and the smallest amounts.

Day	Amount Spent (Dollars)	Amount Saved (Dollars)
Mon		5.80
Tues	88.50	
Wed		2.86
Thurs	72.20	
Fri	94.00	
Sat	46.77	
Sun		1.95

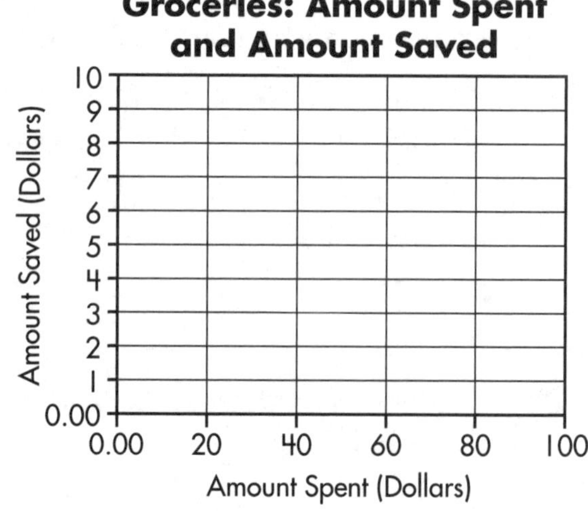

NAME ____________________

Mid-Test Chapters 1–3

Add, subtract, multiply, or divide. Write each answer in simplest form.

	a	b	c	d
1.	$\frac{5}{8} + 1\frac{1}{2}$	$2\frac{1}{5} - 1\frac{2}{3}$	$\frac{3}{16} \times \frac{1}{8} =$	$8\frac{2}{22} \div \frac{2}{3} =$
2.	$7.42 + 2.36 + .09$	$9.54 - 5.32$	6.5×3.3	10.50×6.84
3.	$12.8\overline{)204.80}$	11.432×4.54	$1.7\overline{)29.92}$	$2\frac{3}{16} + 9\frac{1}{5}$

Solve each problem.

4. At her farm, Janet fills $16\frac{2}{3}$ egg cartons with fresh eggs each day. She wants to increase this by $1\frac{3}{4}$ cartons. How many cartons will she fill in one day?

Janet wants to fill __________ cartons per day.

5. Kelly bought a new home for $120,227. Her real estate agent gets 0.075 of the purchase price. How much will she pay the real estate agent? Round up.

Kelly paid __________ to the real estate agent.

6. Rayshawn saved $3,508 to pay rent. His rent is $438.50 per month. His savings will pay the rent for how many months?

Rayshawn's savings will pay the rent for __________ months.

NAME ______________________

Mid-Test Chapters 1–3

Identify the coefficient and the variable in each term below.

	a	b
7.	$4x + 2$	$6 - 2d$
	coefficient ____ variable _____	coefficient ____ variable _____

Underline the operation that should be done first. Then, find the value of the equation.

8. $10 \div (4 + 1) =$ ________________ $(10 - 2) \times 4 + 6$ ________________

Name the property that each equation illustrates. The properties are commutative, associative, identity, or zero.

9. $n \times a = a \times n$ ________________ $0 \div a = 0$ ________________

10. $a \times (w \times y) = (a \times w) \times y$ ____________ $n \times 1 = n$ ________________

Rewrite each expression using the property indicated.

11. identity: $22 \times 1 =$ ________________ zero: $(n + y) \times 0 =$ ________________

12. associative: $5x + (a + b) =$ ____________ commutative: $n + b =$ ____________

Rewrite each expression using the distributive property.

13. $10a + 10b =$ ________________ $a \times (d + b) =$ ________________

Solve the equations.

14. $5n + 4n = 9 \times (5 + 4) =$ ____________ $(8 \times 5) + (n \times 5) = 8 \times (6 + 4) =$ ________

Find the value of the variable in each equation.

	a	b	c
15.	$8 + n = 24$ ________	$25 + x = 125$ ________	$n - 22 = 104$ ________
16.	$10 + x = 45$ ________	$125 - x = 32$ ________	$n - 80 = 224$ ________
17.	$8 \times n = 24$ ________	$n \div 18 = 90$ ________	$a \div 22 = 68$ ________
18.	$a \div 12 = 16$ ________	$12 \times b = 36$ ________	$n \times 8 = 56$ ________

NAME ___________________

Mid-Test Chapters 1–3

Write an equation for each problem. Then, find the value of the variable.

19. Salma began her delivery route with 122 newspapers. When her deliveries were done, she still had 12 newspapers. How many newspapers did she deliver?

_______________ Salma delivered __________ newspapers.

20. Front Street Bakery has 88 boxes of pastries to deliver to restaurants. Each restaurant gets 8 boxes. How many restaurants will receive pastries?

_______________ The bakery delivered pastries to __________ restaurants.

Refer to the graph to answer the questions.

21. What was the sales amount in the best sales month?

____

22. Which two months had about the same sales?

____

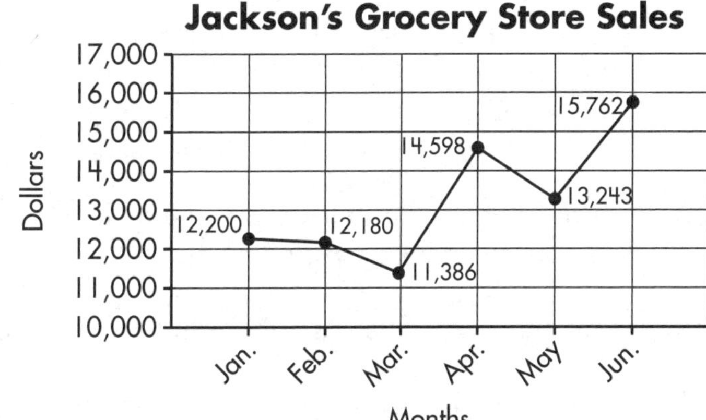

23. Find the lowest value and highest value in the graph. How much did sales rise from its lowest to its highest value? Write an equation for this problem and solve it.

____

Find the unknown number in each proportion.

	a	b	c
24.	$\frac{1}{8} = \frac{n}{16}$ ________	$\frac{n}{30} = \frac{10}{100}$ ________	$\frac{12}{80} = \frac{n}{60}$ ________
25.	$\frac{n}{72} = \frac{4}{12}$ ________	$\frac{8}{56} = \frac{4}{n}$ ________	$\frac{78}{n} = \frac{6}{14}$ ________

NAME ____________________

Mid-Test Chapters 1–3

Add, subtract, multiply, or divide.

	a	b	c
26.	$-7 + 6 =$ ______	$5 + (-2)$ ______	$14 - (-1)$ ______
27.	$-10 \times (-2)$ ______	$60 \div (-5)$ ______	$12 \times (-8)$ ______

Plot each ordered pair on the grid.

28. A (2, 5) B (−7, 4)

29. C (−6, −5) D (7, −4)

30. E (8, 6) F (−3, −2)

31. G (4, −3) H (−4, 2)

32. I (−6, 5) J (5, 7)

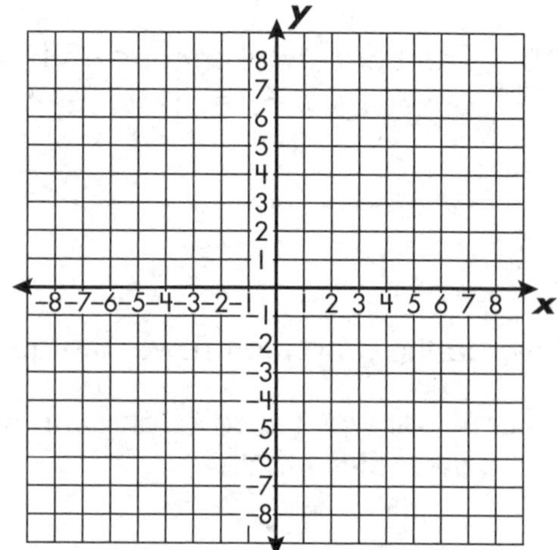

33. Sherri kept track of her car's value as long as she owned it. She recorded the data in the table below. Make a graph of the data.

34. How much was Sherri's car worth when she bought it? ______________

35. In which year did the car lose the most value? ______________

Car Value and Years of Ownership

Years	Car Value (Dollars)
0	30,000
1	26,750
2	24,300
3	21,350
4	18,500
5	14,900
6	14,600

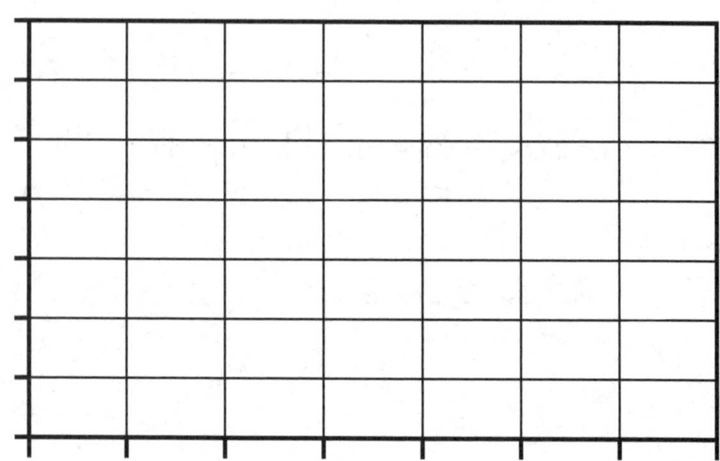

NAME ______________________

Check What You Know

Probability

CHAPTER 4 PRETEST

Solve the problems based on one spin of the spinner. Express each probability as a fraction in simplest form.

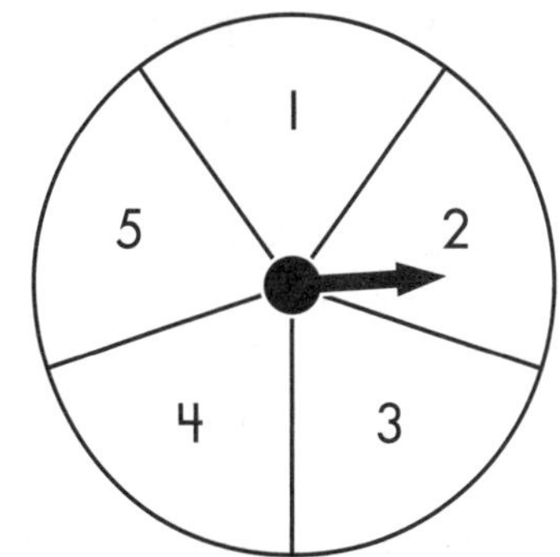

1. The number of possible outcomes is __________.

2. The probability of stopping on 4 is __________.

3. The probability of stopping on an odd number is

__________.

4. The probability of not stopping on an odd number is

__________.

5. The probability of stopping on 5 or 3 is __________.

6. The probability of stopping on a number > 1 is __________.

Solve each problem. Express probabilities as fractions in simplest form.

A bag contains 3 pennies, 2 nickels, and 4 dimes. You will select a coin at random.

7. The probability that you will choose a nickel is __________.

8. The probability that you will choose either a penny or a dime is __________.

9. The probability that you will not choose a penny is __________.

10. The probability that you will choose a coin worth more than 10 cents is __________.

CHAPTER 4 PRETEST

NAME ______________________________

Check What You Know

Probability

Solve each problem. Express each probability as a fraction in simplest form.

A box contains 2 green grapes and 4 purple grapes. Another box contains 3 red balls, 1 white ball, and 3 green balls. You pick one item from each box at random.

11. The probability that you will choose 1 green grape and 1 green ball is __________.

12. The probability that you will choose 1 purple grape and 1 white ball is __________.

The names of 8 girls and 7 boys are written on slips of paper, which are placed in a hat. The teacher will choose names at random to decide the order in which students will present their projects.

13. The probability that a girl will be chosen first and a boy second is _________.

14. The probability that a boy will be chosen first and second is _________.

A snack shop sells hamburgers and turkey burgers with a choice of buns. The tree diagram shows all possible combinations. Use the diagram to answer the questions.

15. There are _______ possible combinations.

16. If you choose a sandwich at random, the probability that you will choose a turkey burger on a wheat bun is

___________.

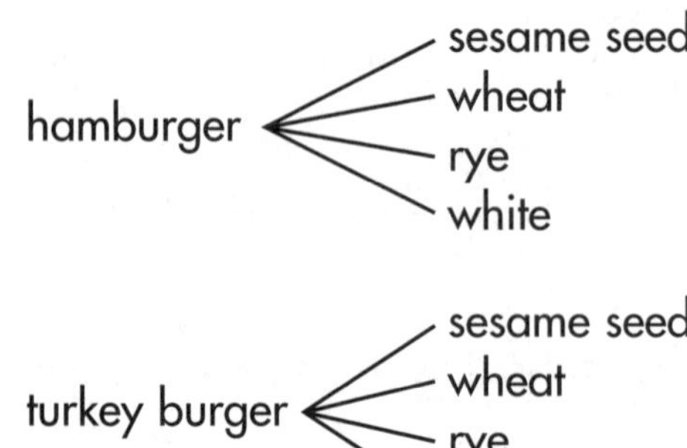

17. The probability that you and your friend will both choose a hamburger on rye is

____________.

NAME ___________________________

Lesson 4.1 Calculating Probability

An **outcome** is a possible result of an activity or experiment. **Probability** is a measure of how likely it is that a specific outcome will occur. To find probability, create a ratio comparing the number of a specific outcome with the total number of possible outcomes.

$$\text{Probability } (P) = \frac{\text{number of a specific outcome}}{\text{number of possible outcomes}}$$

A bag contains 12 marbles: 7 blue and 5 red. If you choose a marble at random, the probability that it will be red is:

$$\text{Probability } (P) = \frac{5}{12} \begin{array}{l} \leftarrow \text{number of a specific outcome} \\ \leftarrow \text{number of possible outcomes} \end{array}$$

You can express probability as a ratio, fraction, decimal, or percent.

When tossing a coin, what is the probability that it will land on heads?

specific outcome: heads

possible outcomes: heads, tails

probability of heads: 1:2, $\frac{1}{2}$, 0.5, or 50%

Find the probability. Express your answer as a fraction in simplest form.

If you spin the spinner at right, what is the probability that the spinner will stop on each of the following?

1. a number ___________

2. an even number ___________

3. an odd number ___________

4. a consonant ___________

5. a vowel ___________

6. the number 6 ___________

7. a number < 6 ___________

8. a number > 6 ___________

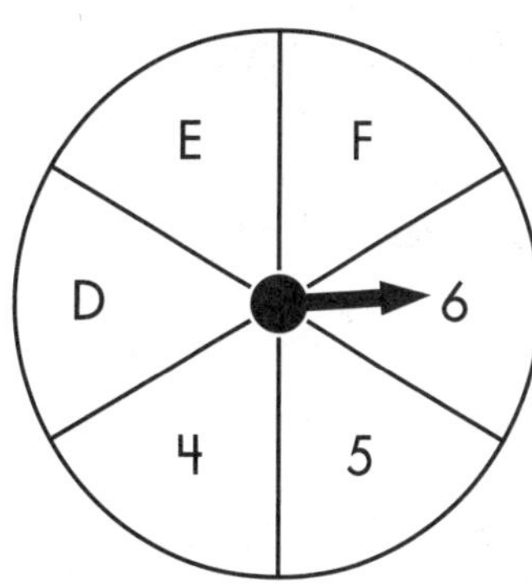

NAME ______________________

Lesson 4.1 Calculating Probability

An **event** is a set of possible outcomes from an activity or experiment. **Sample space** is the set of all possible outcomes of an activity or experiment. An event is a subset of sample space. Suppose you roll a 6-sided die once. The sample space is {1, 2, 3, 4, 5, 6}. You might roll a 2. Thus, one event of this experiment is {2}. If you roll the die twice, you might get a 3 and a 6. Thus, the set {3, 6} is one possible event of rolling the die twice.

Mutually exclusive events are events that cannot occur at the same time. If one event occurs, none of the other events will occur. If you roll a die and get a 6, you cannot get a 1, 2, 3, 4, or 5 at the same time.

If Events A and B are mutually exclusive, then the probability of A *or* B occurring is:

$$P(A) + P(B)$$

In one roll of a die, the probability of getting a 3 is $\frac{1}{6}$ and the probability of getting a 4 is also $\frac{1}{6}$. The probability of getting either a 3 or a 4 in one roll is $\frac{1}{6} + \frac{1}{6} = \frac{2}{6} = \frac{1}{3}$.

Complementary events are events that together make up the entire sample space. The probabilities of complementary events sum to 1, or 100%. Complementary events are mutually exclusive, but not all mutually exclusive events are complementary.

If A' is the complement of A, then the probability of A occurring is:

$$P(A) = 1 - P(A')$$

In one roll of a die, the probability of getting a 3 is $\frac{1}{6}$. Therefore, the probability of not getting a 3 is $1 - \frac{1}{6} = \frac{5}{6}$.

Determine each probability. Express your answer as a fraction in simplest form.

1. On one roll of a 6-sided die, what is the probability of getting a 1, 2, 4, or 6?

The probability of getting a 1, 2, 4, or 6 is ______________________.

2. A bag holds 3 red marbles, 2 green marbles, and 3 black marbles. What is the probability of not choosing a black marble?

The probability of not choosing a black marble is ______________________.

3. Events A and B are mutually exclusive. $P(A) = \frac{3}{10}$. P(B) is $\frac{1}{5}$. What is the probability that either A or B will occur?

P(A) or P(B) is ____________________.

4. Events X, Y, and Z are complementary. $P(X) = \frac{1}{8}$. $P(Y) = \frac{1}{2}$. What is the probability that Z will occur?

P(Z) is ____________________.

NAME ____________________

Lesson 4.1 Calculating Probability

A **compound event** consists of two or more events. Tossing two coins is a compound event. Tossing a coin and rolling a die is also a compound event.

Compound events are **independent** if the outcome of one event does not influence the outcome of the others. When you flip a coin, there is a $\frac{1}{2}$ probability of heads and a $\frac{1}{2}$ probability of tails. Suppose your coin flip produces tails. If you flip the coin again, there is still a $\frac{1}{2}$ probability of heads and a $\frac{1}{2}$ probability of tails. These events are independent.

If events A and B are independent, then the probability of both occurring is:

$P(A) \times P(B)$

The probability of getting tails in one coin flip is $\frac{1}{2}$. The probability of getting a 5 in one roll of a die is $\frac{1}{6}$. The probability of both occurring, {tails, 5}, is $\frac{1}{2} \times \frac{1}{6} = \frac{1}{12}$.

Determine each probability. Express your answer as a fraction in simplest form.

1. Events E and F are independent. The probability that E will occur is $\frac{2}{5}$. The probability that F will occur is $\frac{3}{7}$. What is the probability that both E and F will occur?

   The probability that both E and F will occur is ______________.

2. A nationwide poll found that 3 of 5 voters planned to vote for Candidate X. Jay and Aisha voted. What is the probability that both voted for Candidate X?

   The probability that both voted for Candidate X is ______________.

3. You roll a 6-sided die and flip a coin. What is the probability of getting an even number on the die and heads on the coin?

   P(even) and P(heads) is ________________.

4. A jar of jellybeans has 6 blue, 2 orange, and 8 red jellybeans. You choose 1 jellybean, put it back, and then choose another. What is the probability that you choose 2 blue jellybeans?

   The probability of choosing 2 blue jellybeans is ________________.

NAME ____________________

Lesson 4.1 Calculating Probability

Two events are **dependent** if the outcome of one event influences the outcome of the other. If events A and B are dependent, then the probability of both occurring is:

P(A) × P(B after A occurs)

Suppose a bag holds 2 yellow golf balls and 2 white golf balls. Each color of ball has a $\frac{2}{4}$ or $\frac{1}{2}$ chance of being selected. You take a yellow ball out of the bag and do not replace it. Now, there are 2 white balls and 1 yellow ball. The probability of choosing a white ball next is $\frac{2}{3}$. Therefore, the probability of choosing a yellow ball, P(A), and then a white ball, P(B after A occurs), is $\frac{1}{2} \times \frac{2}{3} = \frac{2}{6} = \frac{1}{3}$.

Determine each probability. Express your answer as a fraction in simplest form.

1. A jar of jellybeans has 6 blue, 2 orange, and 8 red jellybeans. You choose 1 jellybean and eat it. You then choose another and eat it. What is the probability that you ate 2 blue jellybeans?

The probability that you ate 2 blue jellybeans is ____________________.

2. A bowl contains 20 raffle tickets, including 1 winning ticket. You take 1 ticket from the bowl. Your friend then takes 1 ticket from the bowl. What are the chances that both you and your friend picked losing tickets?

The probability of both of you picking losing tickets is ______________.

3. A box holds 5 electronic games. Two of the games are defective. You take 1 game from the box. Without replacing it, you choose another game from the box. How likely is it that you picked 2 defective games?

There is a ______________ probability that both games are defective.

4. A set of 12 cards contains an equal number of clubs, diamonds, hearts, and spades. You take 3 cards from the set. What are the chances that all three are spades?

The probability of 3 spades is ______________.

NAME ____________________

Lesson 4.2 Tree Diagrams

To calculate a probability, you need to know how many outcomes are possible. Recall that the set of all possible outcomes of an activity or experiment is the sample space. To help determine the sample space, organize the possibilities using a list, chart, or tree diagram.

Show the sample space for tossing a nickel, a dime, and a quarter.

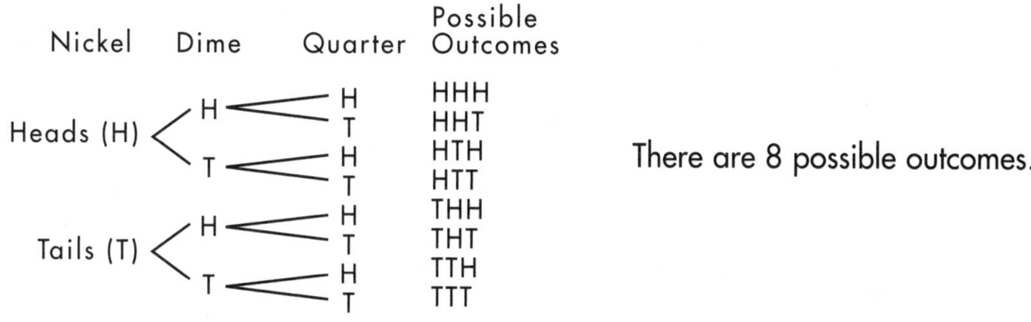

If you tossed these 3 coins once, what is the probability of getting exactly 2 tails? Notice that 3 of the 8 possible outcomes have exactly 2 tails. The probability of getting exactly 2 tails is $\frac{3}{8}$.

Create a tree diagram and answer the question.

1. The chart below shows all possible outcomes of tossing 1 coin and rolling 1 die. In the space provided, create a tree diagram showing all possible outcomes. Begin with the outcomes of the coin toss. Then, connect these outcomes with each possible outcome of the roll of the die.

CHART

Coin

Die	**Heads**	**Tails**
1	H1	T1
2	H2	T2
3	H3	T3
4	H4	T4
5	H5	T5
6	H6	T6

TREE DIAGRAM

Coin **Die**

The number of possible outcomes is __________.

NAME ____________________

Lesson 4.2 Tree Diagrams

Solve each problem. Express probabilities as fractions in simplest form.

1. A store sells T-shirts in the colors and sizes shown in the chart. Make a tree diagram.

Colors	Sizes
red	small
blue	medium
tie-dyed	large

Tree Diagram

a. There are ________ possible outcomes, or choices, of T-shirt.

b. Suppose the store has just 1 of each size and color. If you select a T-shirt at random, the probability that you will choose a large shirt is __________.

2. The tree diagram below shows the combinations of colors, styles, and speeds of bicycles available at a bicycle shop. You select one at random.

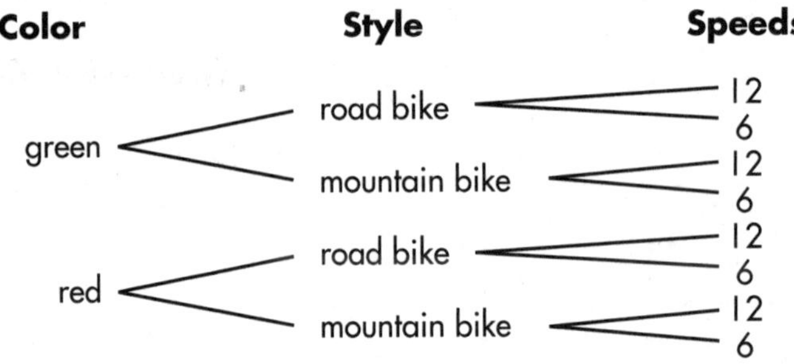

a. There are __________ combinations of bicycles from which to choose.

b. The probability of choosing a green bicycle is __________.

c. The probability of choosing a 6-speed mountain bicycle is __________.

d. The probability of choosing a red, 12-speed road bicycle is __________.

NAME ____________________

Lesson 4.3 Problem Solving

Solve each problem. Write your answer as a fraction in simplest form.

1. You roll a 6-sided die. What is the probability that you will roll a 4?

The probability is ____________________.

2. What is the probability of getting either a 2 or a 5?

The probability is ____________________.

3. What is the probability that you will not roll a 6?

The probability is ____________________.

4. You roll a pair of 6-sided dice once. What is the probability that you will roll two 3s?

The probability is ____________________.

Each of 10 bins contains 1 piece of fruit. Two pieces are oranges, 3 are apples, 4 are peaches, and 1 is a melon. You pick a bin without looking at its contents.

5. What is the probability that you chose an orange?

The probability is ____________________.

6. What is the probability that you chose either an apple or a peach?

The probability is ____________________.

7. You take 1 fruit from a bin and don't replace it. Then you pick another fruit. What is the probability that you chose two peaches?

The probability is ____________________.

8. What is the probability that you did not choose two peaches?

The probability is ____________________.

NAME ____________________

Lesson 4.3 Problem Solving

Solve each problem. Express probabilities as a percent, rounded to the nearest tenth.

1. Jamie will spin the spinner at right 1 time. He will also flip a coin 1 time. Complete the chart of all possible outcomes from this experiment. Two outcomes are given in the chart as examples. Then, draw a tree diagram showing all possible outcomes.

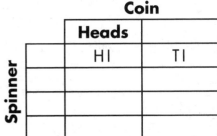

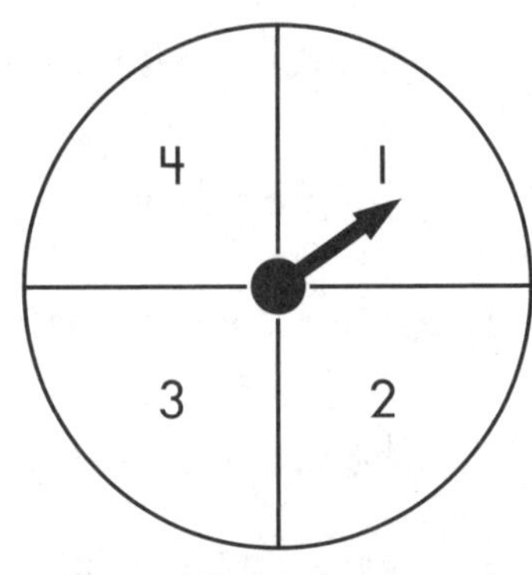

CHART

Coin

Spinner	**Heads**	
	H1	T1

TREE DIAGRAM

Coin **Spinner**

2. This experiment has ____________ possible outcomes.

3. What is the probability of getting heads on the coin flip and 2 on the spin?

The probability is _________%.

4. What is the probability of not getting heads and a 2?

The probability is _________%.

5. What is the probability of getting tails and an odd number?

The probability is _________%.

NAME ______________________

Check What You Learned

Probability

Solve each problem. Express probabilities as fractions in simplest form.

A deck of playing cards has 52 cards and 4 suits: clubs, diamonds, hearts, and spades. Each suit has an equal number of cards. The cards range from 2 through ace in each suit. You draw 1 card at random. What is the probability that the card is:

1. a jack? ________

2. a club? ________

3. either an ace or a diamond? ________

4. not a spade? ________

You draw 1 card at random, replace it, and then draw another card. What is the probability that you drew:

5. a king and a 9? ________

6. a spade and a heart? ________

7. a 2 and a diamond? ________

You draw 1 card at random and do *not* replace it. You then draw another card. What is the probability that you drew:

8. a queen and then a 5? ________

9. a club and then a spade? ________

CHAPTER 4 POSTTEST

NAME ______________________________

Check What You Learned

Probability

Solve each problem. Express probabilities as fractions in simplest form.

You are serving cheese at a party. The tray holds 6 cheddar cubes, 5 Swiss cubes, and 8 provolone cubes. If each person chooses 1 cube at random, what is the probability that:

10. both the first and second person chose cheddar? ________

11. the first person chose Swiss and the second chose provolone? ________

12. At a restaurant, you can choose a chicken, steak, or fish dinner. With each dinner you have a choice of a salad or fruit. Each dinner also comes with rice or a potato. If you choose a dinner at random, create a tree diagram showing all possible outcomes.

Use your tree diagram to answer the following questions. Express probabilities as percents, rounded to the nearest tenth.

13. How many possible outcomes are there? ________

What is the probability of choosing a dinner with:

14. fruit? ________%

15. steak and potato? ________%

16. fish, salad, and rice? ________%

NAME ____________________

Check What You Know

Measures of Central Tendency

Find the mean, median, mode, and range of each set of data. Round to the nearest tenth.

1.

a	**b**	**c**
8, 9, 4, 2, 9	25, 17, 14, 29, 17, 24	6, 4, 0, 2, 5, 7, 1, 3
mean: ________	mean: ________	mean: ________
median: ________	median: ________	median: ________
mode: ________	mode: ________	mode: ________
range: ________	range: ________	range: ________

2. Dana scored 80, 86, 79, and 81 on her first 4 math quizzes. What score does she need on the fifth quiz to reach an average of 84?

a. Equation: ____________________ **b.** Dana needs a score of ________.

3. Kerry's Berries sold a mean of 24 quarts of blueberries per day. The store sold a total of 720 quarts during the sample period. How many days are in the sample?

a. Equation: ____________________ **b.** The sample has ________ days.

The stem-and-leaf plot represents a set of data. Use the plot to answer the questions.

4. Which numbers in the set are in the 30–39 interval? ________

5. What is the mode of the set? ________

6. What is the median of the set? ________

7. What is the lowest number in the set? ________

8. What is the range of the set? ________

Stem	Leaves
2	1 4
3	2 5 7
4	1 3 4 9
5	6 6 8
6	1 1 1

Key: 2 | 1 = 21

NAME ____________________

Check What You Know

Measures of Central Tendency

9. A car dealer surveyed customers to find out the color of car they prefer. Survey responses are shown in the frequency table. Complete the table. Round to tenths.

Popularity of Colors for Cars			
Color	**Frequency**	**Cumulative Frequency**	**Relative Frequency**
red	25		%
blue	20		%
black	16		%
silver	43		%
white	36		%

10. How many customers responded to the survey? ________

11. What color was most popular? ________

12. What percentage of customers preferred blue or white? ________%

Use the line plot to answer the questions.

13. What is the mode? ________

14. What is the range? ________

15. How many years does the plot include? ________

16. What is the median? ________

Tornadoes per Year in a State

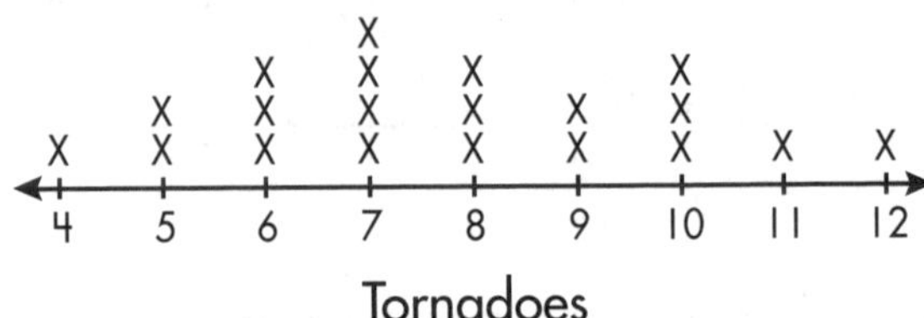

Use the box-and-whisker plot to answer the questions.

17. What is the median? ________

18. What is the upper quartile? ________

19. What is the interquartile range? ________

Number of Movies Watched over Summer

0 2 4 6 8 10 12 14 16 18

Movies

NAME ______________________

Lesson 5.1 Measures of Central Tendency

Mean, median, and mode are measures of central tendency. You can use these measures to analyze sets of data.

The **mean** is the average of a set of numbers. To find the mean, add all the numbers in the set and divide by the number of addends.

The **median** is the middle number of a set of numbers. If the set contains an even number of values, the median is the mean, or average, of the two middle numbers.

The **mode** is the most frequent number—the number that appears most often in a set of numbers. A set can have no mode, one mode, or more than one mode. If all the numbers in a set occur the same number of times, the set has no mode. If two or more numbers appear most often, then each of those numbers is a mode of that set.

Find the mean of the set 12, 15, 18, 23, 8, 10, 12.

mean: $12 + 15 + 18 + 23 + 8 + 10 + 12 = 98$ $\frac{98}{7} = 14$

To find the median and mode, arrange the numbers in order: 8, 10, 12, 12, 15, 18, 23

median: 12 mode: 12

Find the median of 8, 6, 5, 7, 2, 10. First, order the numbers: 2, 5, 6, 7, 8, 10

The middle numbers are 6 and 7. median: $\frac{6+7}{2} = \frac{13}{2} = 6\frac{1}{2}$

Find the mean, median, and mode of each set of numbers.

	a	b
1.	25, 20, 14, 25, 16	32, 36, 21, 19, 21, 36
	mean: ________	mean: ________
	median: ________	median: ________
	mode: ________	mode: ________
2.	23, 8, 2, 11, 65, 6, 4	5, 13, 0, 45, 80, 0, 5, 0
	mean: ________	mean: ________
	median: ________	median: ________
	mode: ________	mode: ________

NAME ____________________

Lesson 5.1 Measures of Central Tendency

Another way to examine a set of data is to look at how spread out the data is. Range is a measure of spread. The **range** of a set of numbers is the difference between the greatest and least numbers in the set.

Find the mean and range of these sets of data.

Set A: 60, 64, 59, 57, 60

order the numbers: 57, 59, 60, 60, 64

range: 64 – 57 = 7

mean: $\frac{300}{5} = 60$

Set B: 52, 35, 75, 110, 28

order the numbers: 28, 35, 52, 75, 110

range: 110 – 28 = 82

mean: $\frac{300}{5} = 60$

Both sets of data have a mean of 60. However, Set B has a larger range than Set A. The larger range means that the data are more spread out in Set B than in Set A.

The following table lists test scores for 3 students. Use the table to answer the questions.

Student	Test 1	Test 2	Test 3	Test 4	Test 5
Cory	88	93	81	97	84
Kara	85	84	84	86	83
Suki	90	92	88	85	92

1. Write Cory's scores in order: ____________________

Cory's mean: ________ median: ________ mode: ________ range: ________

2. Write Kara's scores in order: ____________________

Kara's mean: ________ median: ________ mode: ________ range: ________

3. Write Suki's scores in order: ____________________

Suki's mean: ________ median: ________ mode: ________ range: ________

4. Which student performed most consistently on the tests? Explain how you know.

____

NAME ____________________

Lesson 5.1 Measures of Central Tendency

Each measure of central tendency provides a useful, but different, way to analyze sets of data. The mean evens out, or balances, a set of data. The mean is a good way to describe the middle of a set of data that does not have an outlier. An **outlier** is an extreme value, a number that is much larger or smaller than the other numbers in the set.

The median is a good way to describe the middle of a set that does have an outlier. An outlier affects the median less than the mean. The mode is useful for data that are not numbers. For example, you might use the mode to identify the most popular item in a set.

Consider this ordered set: 9, 9, 10, 10, 14, 35 mean = 87 ÷ 6 = 14.5 median = 10

The number 35 is much higher than the other numbers. What if we remove the outlier?

Set with outlier removed: 9, 9, 10, 10, 14 mean = 52 ÷ 5 = 10.4 median = 10

Without the outlier, the mean declined significantly, but the median was not affected.

The hourly wages of employees at two stores are shown below. Use measures of central tendency to analyze the data. Round to the nearest cent.

	a **Sam's Pet World**	b **Beth's Pets**
Hourly wages ($)	10, 9.5, 8.25, 9, 10, 9.5, 8.5, 10.5	9.25, 8, 7.5, 8.5, 7.75, 20, 8, 9
1. mean	$________	$________
2. median	$________	$________
3. mode	$________	$________

4. Which store do you think pays its employees better? Explain your answer.

____

____

5. Suppose you are Beth. You want to convince a potential employee that you pay your employees well. What measure of central tendency would you use? Why?

____

NAME ______________________

Lesson 5.1 Measures of Central Tendency

Sometimes you may know the mean and need to find a missing piece of data. You can use equations to solve for the missing number.

Midori has these scores on three math tests: 88, 92, 94. Midori wants to know what score she needs on the fourth test to bring her average up to 92.

Mean:	$\frac{88 + 92 + 94 + n}{4} = 92$	n = the score on the fourth test
	$\frac{274 + n}{4} = 92$	simplify
	$274 + n = 368$	multiply each side by 4
	$n = 94$	subtract 274 from each side

Midori must get a 94 on the fourth test to bring her average up to 92.

Use an equation to find the missing number in each problem. Show your work.

1. In six basketball games, Diego scored 14, 16, 11, 18, 12, and 17 points. By the end of the next game, Diego wants his average to be 15 points per game. How many points must Diego score in the seventh game to achieve his goal?

Diego must score ________ points.

2. The mean temperature in an area is 74 degrees Fahrenheit. The sum of the temperatures is 2,516. How many temperatures are in the set?

There are ________ temperatures in the set.

3. The mean of 25 prices is $11.40. What is the sum of the set of prices?

The sum of the set is $ ________.

NAME ______________________

Lesson 5.2 Frequency Tables

Frequency is the number of times a value occurs in a data set. **Cumulative frequency** is the sum of all frequencies up to and including the current one. **Relative frequency** is frequency expressed as a percent or fraction of the total.

Make a frequency table for these test scores:

71, 85, 73, 92, 86, 79, 87, 98, 82, 93, 81, 89, 88, 96

Step 1: Order the scores: 71, 73, 79, 81, 82, 85, 86, 87, 88, 89, 92, 93, 96, 98

Step 2: Make reasonable intervals. Here, intervals are 5 points.

Step 3: Sum the frequencies in each interval for the Frequency column.

Step 4: Calculate cumulative frequencies by adding the frequency of each interval to the previous total.

Test Scores			
Score	**Frequency**	**Cumulative Frequency**	**Relative Frequency**
71–75	2	2	14.3%
76–80	1	3	7.1%
81–85	3	6	21.4%
86–90	4	10	28.6%
91–95	2	12	14.3%
96–100	2	14	14.3%

Step 5: Calculate relative frequencies as percents or fractions of the total items in the set, which is the last cumulative frequency.

Complete the frequency table. Calculate relative frequencies as fractions in simplest form and as percents rounded to the nearest tenth. Then, answer the questions.

Pet Ownership				
Number of Pets	**Frequency**	**Cumulative Frequency**	**Relative Frequency (fraction)**	**Relative Frequency (percent)**
0	8	8		%
1	29	37		%
2	15	52		%
3	6	58		%
4+	2	60		%

1. How many people were polled? ________

2. What fraction of the people polled have 2 or 3 pets? ________

NAME ______________________

Lesson 5.2 Frequency Tables

Fill in the missing numbers in the frequency table. Then, answer the questions.

Points Scored per Basketball Game			
Points	**Frequency**	**Cumulative Frequency**	**Relative Frequency**
30–39		3	$\frac{1}{10}$
40–49		8	
50–59		16	
60–69		26	
70–79		30	

1. How many games does this data cover? ________

2. How many points are in each interval? ________

Use the following data to complete the frequency table and answer the questions.

Heights of students in a class, in feet: 5.2, 5.6, 4.6, 6.0, 5.4, 5.1, 4.6, 5.2, 5.9, 6.1, 5.5, 5.2, 5.8, 5.3, 5.6, 5.9, 5.4, 5.7, 5.4, 4.8.

3. Arrange the heights in order, from lowest to highest: ______________________

____

Heights of Students in a Class			
Height, in Feet	**Frequency**	**Cumulative Frequency**	**Relative Frequency**
4.5–4.9			%
5.0–5.4			%
5.5–5.9			%
6.0–6.5			%

4. How many students are in the class? ________

5. The heights of most of the students fall within what interval? ________ feet.

6. What percent of the students are 6 feet tall or taller? ________%

7. What percent of the students are less than 6 feet tall? ________%

NAME ____________________

Lesson 5.3 Stem-and-Leaf Plots

A **stem-and-leaf plot** is a way to organize data to examine the shape. Stem-and-leaf plots display the data in two columns, using place values. The right column shows the **leaves**—the "ones" digit of each number. The other digits are the **stems**, which appear in the left column. The key explains how to read the plot.

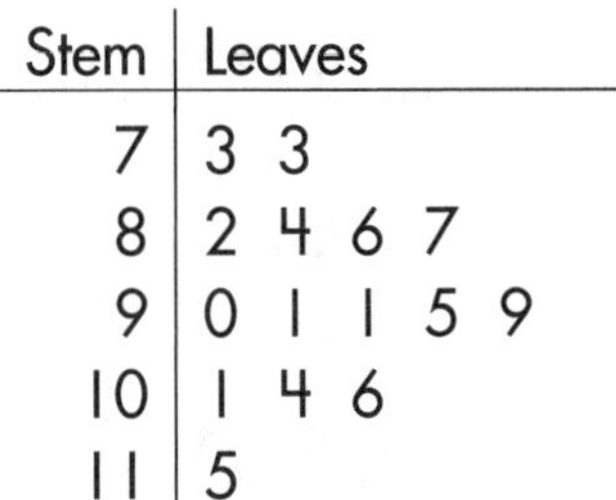

Stem	Leaves
7	3 3
8	2 4 6 7
9	0 1 1 5 9
10	1 4 6
11	5

Key: 7 | 1 = 71

Use the following data to create a stem-and-leaf plot:

82, 95, 115, 84, 91, 87, 90, 104, 86, 91, 73, 99, 101, 73, 106

Step 1: Arrange the numbers in order, from least to greatest. 73, 73, 82, 84, 86, 87, 90, 91, 91, 95, 99, 101, 104, 106, 115

Step 2: Make a vertical list of stems, from the lowest "tens" digit to the highest digit. Use a vertical line to separate the stem and leaves.

Step 3: List each "ones" digit next to its stem.

Step 4: Add a key that tells how to read the plot.

The lengths of the leaves give you a sense of the shape and spread of the data. To see these characteristics, visualize the plot turned sideways, as shown at right. The data have been enclosed in bars to help you visualize. The height of each leaf column shows the shape of the data.

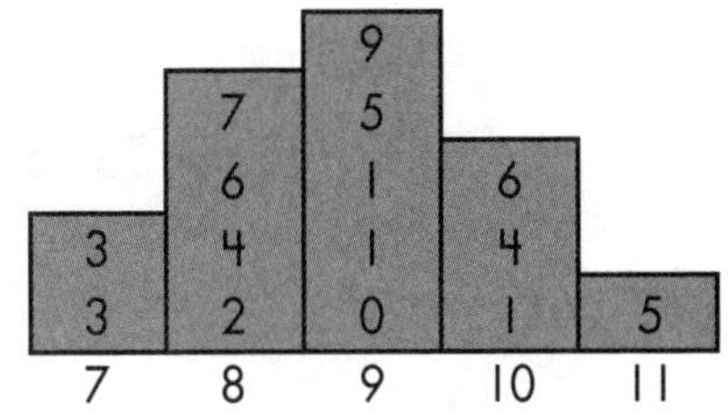

Use the stem-and-leaf plot above to answer these questions.

1. What is the mode of this data? ________

2. What is the highest number in this data set? ________

3. What is the lowest number in this data set? ________

4. What is the range? ________

NAME ____________________

Lesson 5.3 Stem-and-Leaf Plots

Unlike frequency tables, stem-and-leaf plots keep the raw data. For example, a frequency table might show that 3 numbers in the set fall in the 30–39 interval. However, the table does not tell you the exact numbers. A stem-and-leaf plot gives the numbers:

Stem	Leaves
3	4 8

The numbers in the 30–39 range are 34 and 38.

Create a stem-and-leaf plot and key for each set of data. Then, answer the questions.

1. 46, 29, 35, 44, 29, 26, 55, 46, 53, 27, 32, 31, 22

Key: ________

Stem	Leaves

2. 441, 432, 455, 435, 469, 451, 442, 469, 451, 443, 455

Key: ________

Stem	Leaves

3. Chicago, Illinois posted the following high temperatures (in degrees Fahrenheit) for the month of April: 83, 81, 59, 76, 72, 76, 49, 40, 56, 74, 63, 70, 63, 80, 82, 68, 59, 52, 56, 64, 62, 60, 63, 60, 60, 63, 46, 59, 70, 74

Key: ________

Stem	Leaves

4. What was the mode for Chicago in April? ________ degrees

5. What was the range of high temperatures for the month? ________ degrees

6. What temperature was the median for the month? ________ degrees

NAME ______________________

Lesson 5.4 Line Plots

A **line plot** is a graph that shows frequency of data on a number line. Line plots make it easy to identify the mode, range, and any outliers. Recall that an outlier is an extreme value, a number that is much larger or smaller than the other numbers in the set.

To make a line plot, draw a number line from the least to the greatest value in the number set. Then, make an X above each number every time it appears in the set. The number of Xs above each number shows how many times that number appears—its frequency.

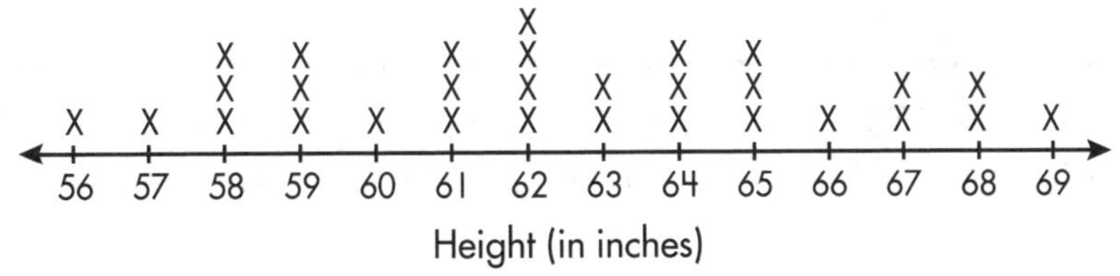

What is the mode, or most frequent height? Look for the tallest stack of Xs. The mode is 62 inches. What is the range of heights in the class? Subtract the least height from the greatest: 69 – 56 = 13 inches. How many students were polled? Count the total number of Xs. Thirty students were polled. What is the median height of the students? Count 15 Xs in from the left and 15 Xs in from the right. The median is the average of these two numbers. Because both numbers are 62 inches, the median is 62 inches.

The Eagles baseball team scored these numbers of runs per game: 4, 2, 6, 3, 1, 0, 2, 0, 4, 5, 0, 7, 6, 4, 3, 2, 6, 8, 1, 3, 11, 7, 3. Make a line plot. Then, answer the questions.

1. What is the mode? ________ What is the range? ________

2. How many games did the Eagles play? ________ What is the median? ________

3. If there is an outlier, identify it. ________

NAME ____________________

Lesson 5.4 Line Plots

Line plots can also help you see clusters and gaps in the data. Clusters are groups of points separated from other points. Gaps are large spaces between points.

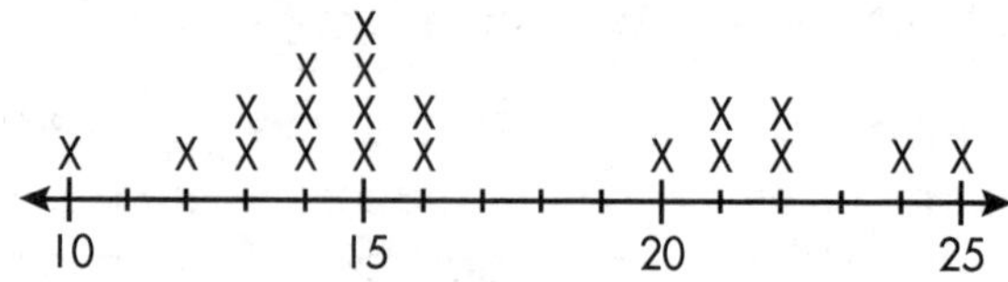

The largest clusters of data in the plot lie in the 12 through 16 range and the 20 through 22 range. The largest gap is 17 through 19.

As a store manager, you collected data on the average number of transactions that each sales clerk handled in a day. Use the plot of the data below to answer the questions.

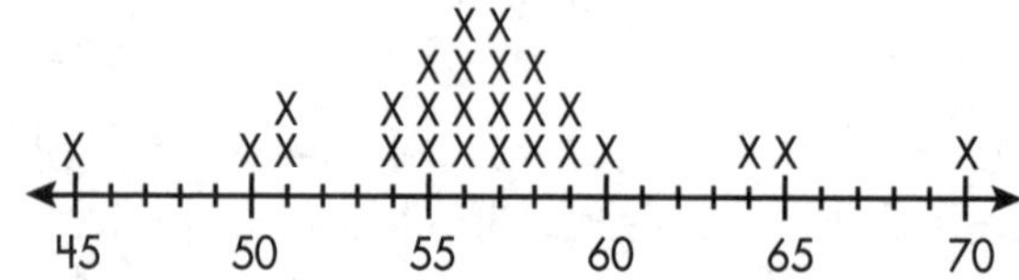

1. What is the mode? ________

2. What is the data range? ________

3. How many sales clerks does the store employ? ________

4. What is the median number of transactions? ________

5. Based on the data, what range of transactions would you consider a standard day's work for a sales clerk? Explain why.

____

6. Above what number of transactions would you consider giving an award for employee of the month? Explain your reasoning.

____

NAME ______________________

Lesson 5.5 Box-and-Whisker Plots

A **box-and-whisker plot** displays data along a number line, using quartiles. Quartiles are numbers that divide the data into quarters, or 4 equal parts. The median, or middle quartile, divides the data in half. The lower quartile is the median of the lower half of the data. The upper quartile is the median of the upper half of the data.

Twenty-five percent of the data lies between quartiles. The upper and lower quartiles, enclosing 50% of the data, form the box. The upper extreme (highest value) and lower extreme (lowest value) form the whiskers.

To draw a box-and-whisker plot, first arrange the data in order:

12, 13, 14, 14, 15, 16, 17, 18, 19, 19, 21

Lower Extreme, Lower Quartile, Median, Upper Quartile, Upper Extreme

12 13 14 15 16 17 18 19 20 21

Middle Quartile (median): 16
Upper Extreme: 21
Lower Extreme: 12

Upper Quartile (median of upper half): 19
Lower Quartile (median of lower half): 14

Use the box-and-whisker plot below to answer the following questions.

Miles Ridden in a Bike-a-Thon

10 15 20 25 30 35 40 45 50

1. The most miles ridden were ________.

2. The fewest miles ridden were ________.

3. Half the riders rode ________ miles or more.

4. If 80 riders participated, how many people rode 40–45 miles? ________

The scores on a quiz were 5, 10, 15, 25, 30, 35, 40.

5. What is the median of these scores? ________

6. What is the lower quartile? ________ What is the upper quartile? ________

7. Using the number line below, draw a box-and-whisker plot for these scores.

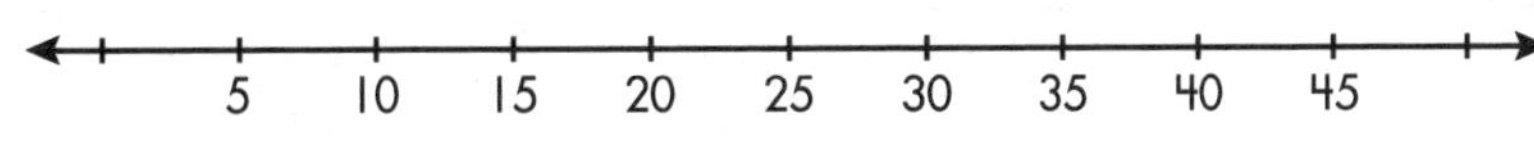

NAME ____________________

Lesson 5.5 Box-and-Whisker Plots

A box-and-whisker plot does not show the number of data points. As a result, you cannot use this kind of plot to find the mean or mode. A box-and-whisker plot helps you see at a glance the center, the spread, and the overall range of the data.

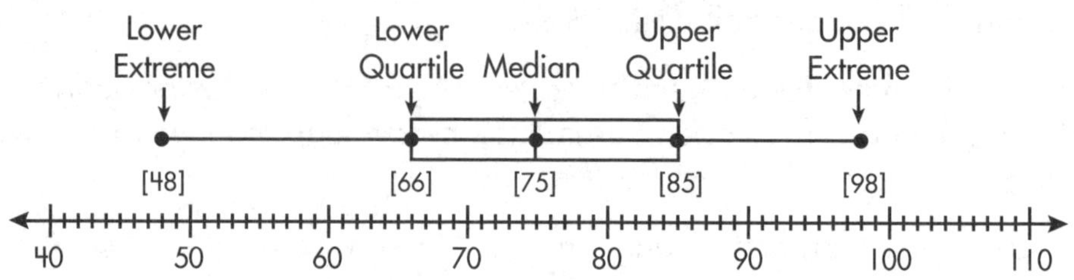

To find the range of the set, subtract the lower extreme from the upper extreme: 98 – 48 = 50. The **interquartile range** is the range of the middle 50% of the data. To find the interquartile range, subtract the lower quartile from the upper quartile: 85 – 66 = 19.

Use the box-and-whiskers plots below to answer the questions.

Hourly Wages at XYZ Company

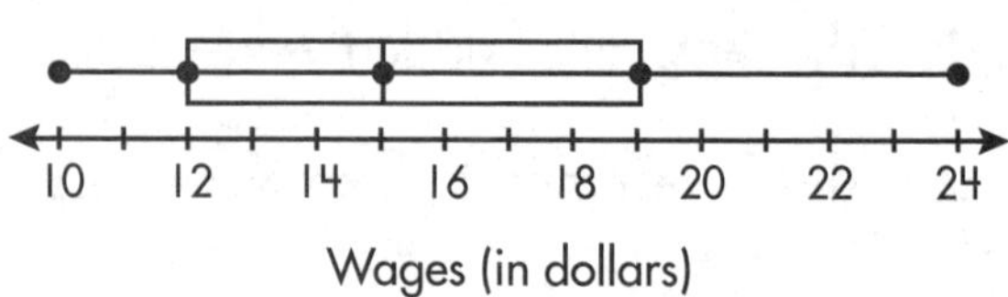

1. The range of wages is ________.

2. The interquartile range is ________

3. The pay for the top 50% of workers ranges from $ ________ to ________.

4. Are wages more spread out for the top 50% or bottom 50% of workers? ________

How can you tell by looking at the plot? ____________________

Passengers per Flight from Airport X

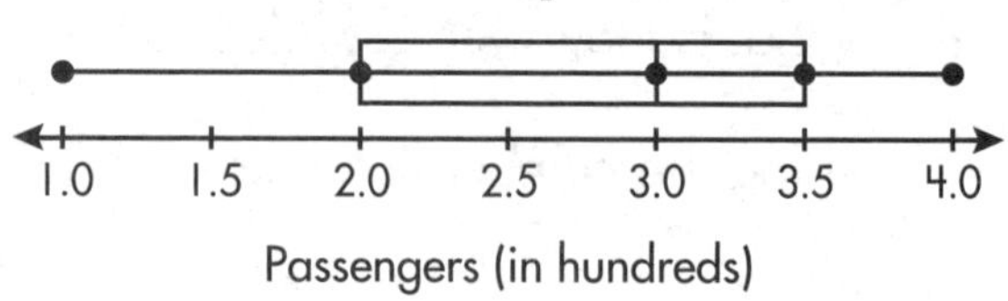

5. The range of passengers is ________.

6. What range of passengers does the middle 50% of flights carry? ________

7. Is it likely that most planes that fly from Airport X can hold at least 300 passengers?

Explain your answer. ____________________

NAME ____________________

Lesson 5.6 Problem Solving

The table shows the weights of players on a football team, in pounds. Use this table to answer the questions. Round to the nearest pound.

Team Roster	
Player	**Weight (lb.)**
Smith	250
Lawson	205
Stone	280
Reyes	200
Stein	280
Kwan	275
Turner	220
Rockwell	280
Koros	210
Manoa	300
Jones	250
Wilson	210

1. What is the mean? ________ pounds

2. What is the mode? ________ pounds

3. What is the median? ________ pounds

A player who weighs 150 pounds joined the team.

4. Now what is the mean? ________ pounds

5. What is the mode? ________ pounds

6. What is the median? ________ pounds

7. Which measure of central tendency was most influenced by the addition of an extreme value?

____

Suppose instead of a 150-pound player, the team added a 350-pound player to the roster.

8. What would happen to the mean? ________________________________

9. What would happen to the mode? ________________________________

10. What would happen to the median? ________________________________

Suppose you are writing the media guide for the team shown in the table. You want to impress readers with how big your team is. Use the proper measurements to complete these statements for the guide:

11. "Half of our players weigh ________ pounds or more."

12. "We have more players who weigh ________ pounds than any other weight."

NAME ______________________

Lesson 5.6 Problem Solving

The box-and-whisker plots and the stem-and-leaf plots on this page compare the average high temperatures for Cleveland, Ohio, and Seattle, Washington, throughout the year. Use the plots to answer the questions.

Average High Temperature in Cleveland

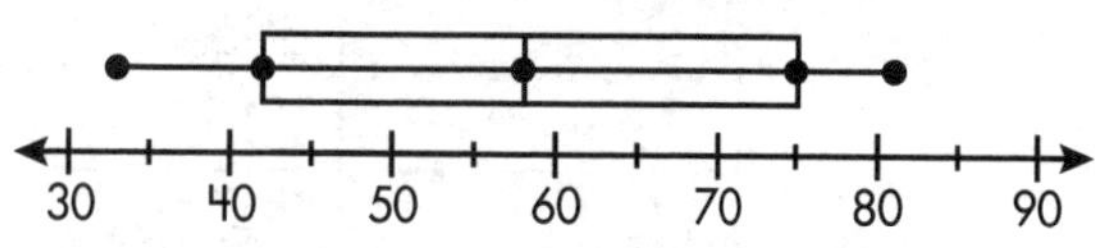

Average High Temperature in Seattle

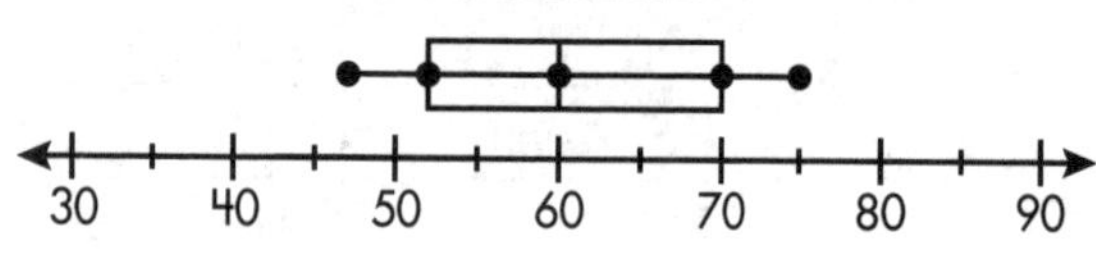

Average High Temperatures in °F (rounded)

Cleveland Leaves	Stem	Seattle Leaves
3 6 7	3	
6 9	4	7 7
7	5	1 2 5
1 9	6	0 0 5
2 7 9	7	0 0 5 5
1	8	

1. Which city has the mildest climate? ______________

   a. How can you tell from the box-and-whisker plots?

   ____

   b. How can you tell from the stem-and-leaf plots?

   ____

2. Which city experiences the greatest seasonal temperature changes? ______________

   a. How can you tell from the box-and-whisker plots?

   ____

   b. How can you tell from the stem-and leaf plots?

   ____

Compare the box-and-whisker and stem-and-leaf plots. Which would you use to compare:

3. the means? ________
4. the medians? ________
5. the modes? ________
6. the data spread? ________

NAME ____________________

Check What You Learned

Measures of Central Tendency

Find the mean, median, mode, and range of each set of data. Round to the nearest tenth.

1.

a	b	c
22, 18, 3, 32, 18, 44	48, 15, 0, 23, 0, 2, 113	3, 12, 4, 3, 15, 4, 20, 12
mean: ______	mean: ______	mean: ______
median: ______	median: ______	median: ______
mode: ______	mode: ______	mode: ______
range: ______	range: ______	range: ______

2. Chris has these bowling scores: 130, 135, 129, 133. Then, she bowled a 165. Will this new score have the most effect on the mean, median, or mode? ______

3. Menendez Realty sold 24, 20, 26, 14, 18 houses each month. How many houses does the company need to sell to average 20 sales for the 6-month period?

a. Equation: ____________ b. The company must sell ______ houses.

4. The mean of 24 temperatures is 65°F. What is the sum of the set of temperatures?

a. Equation: ____________ b. The temperatures total ______°F.

5. Make a stem-and-leaf plot from this set of data: 236, 222, 267, 227, 239, 235, 251, 243, 256, 260, 244. Include a key. Use the plot to answer the questions.

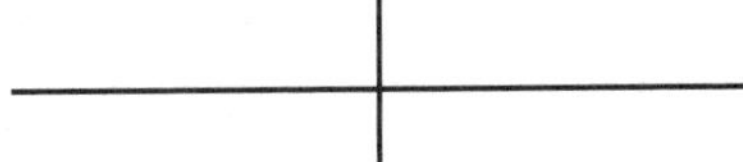

6. What is the mode of the set? ______

7. What is the median of the set? ______

8. What is the lowest number in the set? ______

9. What is the range of the set? ______

CHAPTER 5 POSTTEST

NAME ______________________

Check What You Learned

Measures of Central Tendency

The times for the top finishers of a 10K race are, in minutes: 32, 34, 41, 35, 42, 46, 30, 44, 42, 34, 37, 44, 45, 44, 43. Use this data to answer the questions. Round to tenths.

10. Complete the frequency table.

Minutes	Frequency	Cumulative Frequency	Relative Frequency
30–34			%
35–39			%
40–44			%
45–49			%

11. Make a line plot to display this data.

12. Make a box-and-whisker plot for this data.

Find the following values from the data above.

	a	b
13.	mean: ________	range: ________
14.	median: ________	upper extreme: ________
15.	mode: ________	lower extreme: ________
16.	lower quartile: ________	interquartile range: ________

NAME ________________

Check What You Know

Creating and Interpreting Graphs

1. The sectors on the circle graph below were created from the data table. In the table, complete the percent and degrees columns. Then, complete the graph by including a graph title and sector labels. Match each country to the correct sector by measuring with a protractor, if necessary.

Annual Product Exports			
Country	**Sales (millions)**	**%**	**Degrees**
Germany	$12		
Great Britain	16		
France	10		
Canada	7		
China	4		
Korea	1		
Total:	**$50**		

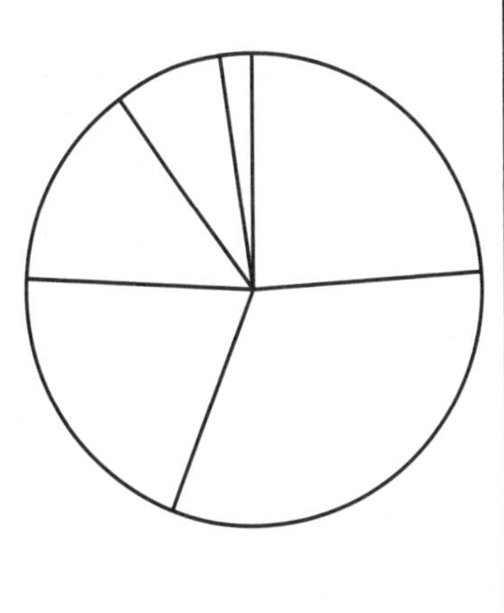

Refer to the graph to answer the following questions.

2. What does the graph show?

____

____

3. What interval is shown by each bar?

____

4. Which age group has the greatest number of investment dollars? ________

5. What information is shown on the frequency axis in this histogram? ________

6. Which age category has $10.5 million in investments? ________

Trustworthy Investments, Inc.
Investments by Age Group

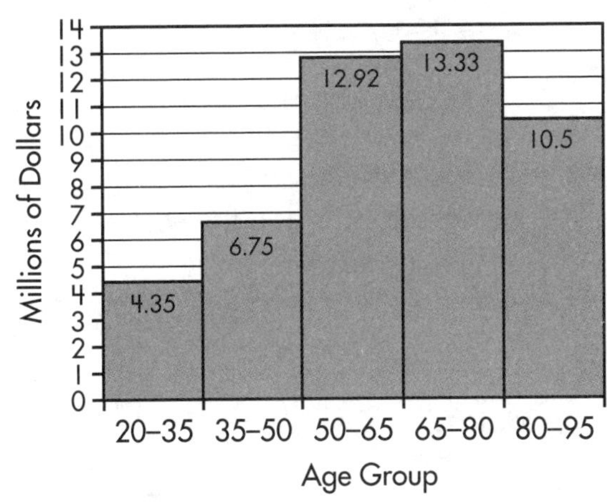

NAME ______________________

Check What You Know

Creating and Interpreting Graphs

7. An animal shelter collected the data in the table below. Using the blank graph provided, create a multiple bar graph from the data table.

Animal Shelter Dog Adoptions			
	Under 20 lb.	**20-50 lb.**	**Over 50 lb.**
Oct.	18	14	12
Nov.	22	16	14
Dec.	28	19	18
Jan.	8	5	9
Feb.	17	18	4

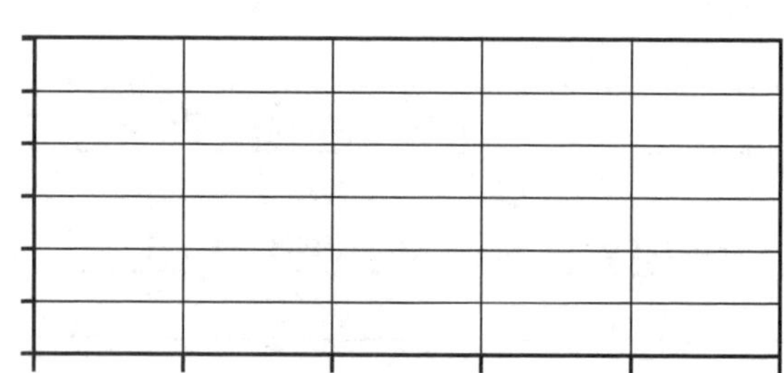

8. What does the multiple line graph on the right show?

____

____

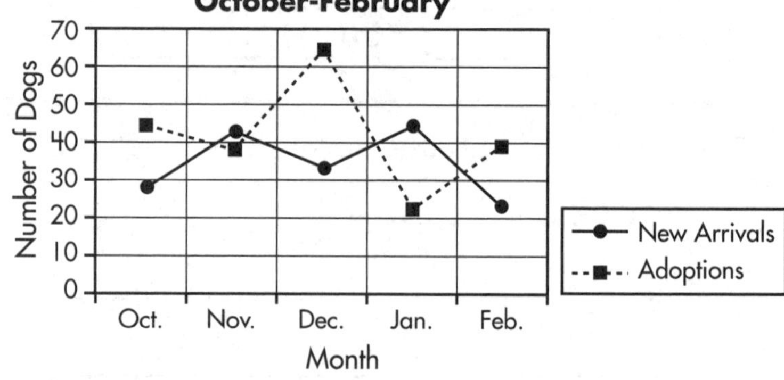

9. In which months did the shelter have more new arrivals than adoptions?

____

10. Describe the variables that are being compared in the scatterplot.

____

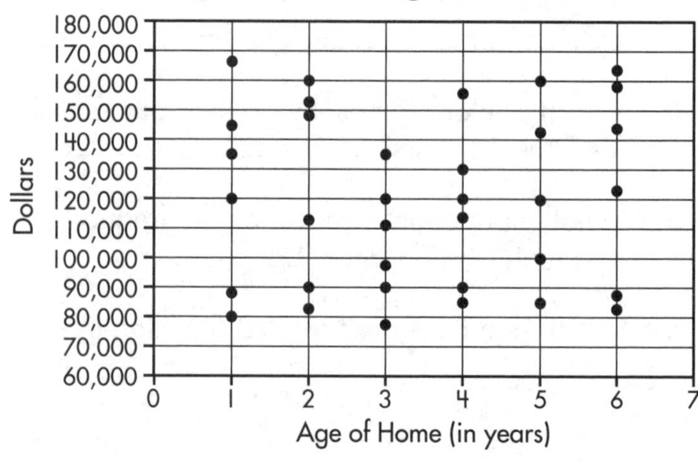

11. Is there an apparent pattern in the data?

____

12. Does the scatterplot show a positive correlation, a negative correlation, or no correlation?

____

NAME ________________

Lesson 6.1 Bar Graphs

A **bar graph** compares data collected from two or more sets of data. The vertical bar graph below was created from the sets of data shown in the table. A bar graph is intended to provide an overview of the data. The table presents the exact information.

There are two axes on a bar graph. The **group data axis** is at the base of the bars. In the graph below, the group data axis shows months. The **frequency axis** measures the frequency, or the amounts of the data. In the graph below, the frequency axis shows the units or number of bicycles sold. The scale on the frequency axis is determined by the range of the data. The data range is from 38 to 450. To contain this range, the scale runs from 0 to 500.

Rick's Bike Shop	
Month	**Bicycles Sold**
Jan.	40
Feb.	38
Mar.	110
Apr.	212
May	420
Jun.	450
Jul.	332
Aug.	313
Sep.	130
Oct.	109
Nov.	90
Dec.	340

Refer to the table and graph above to answer the following questions.

1. In which month did Rick's Bike Shop sell the most bikes? ________

In which month did the shop sell the fewest bikes? ________

2. How many bikes did the shop sell from April through August? ________

What percentage is this of total units sold for the year? ________

3. How many bikes did the shop sell from September through March? ________

What percentage is this of total units sold for the year? ________

NAME ______________________

Lesson 6.1 Bar Graphs

A multiple bar graph allows you to compare two or more sets of data. The graph below shows three sets of data for each month. The graph was created from the data shown in the table.

Notice the key at the bottom of the graph. It identifies the data categories (the bars). This multiple bar graph appears in a horizontal format. It could also appear in a vertical format with the group data axis (the months) at the bottom of the graph and the frequency axis (the units) on the side of the graph.

Bicycle Sales by Price Category, May-August

Month	Over $400	$200–$399	Under $200	Totals
May	182	102	136	**420**
June	152	188	110	**450**
July	166	120	46	**332**
August	175	110	28	**313**
Totals	**675**	**520**	**320**	**1,515**

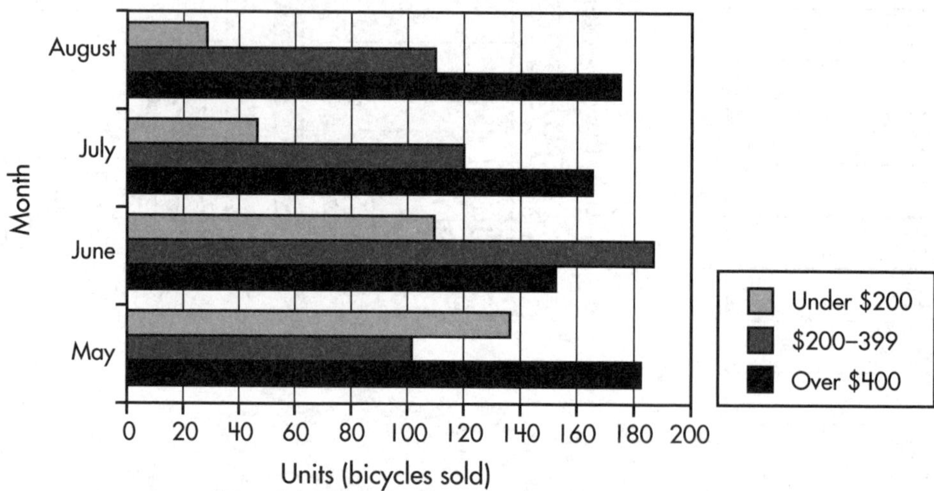

Refer to the table and graph above to answer the following questions.

1. Which three categories of data are shown for each month?

____

2. **a.** Which category sold the most units from May through August? ________

   b. How many total units were sold in this category? ________

3. From May through August, what percentage of total units sold was under $200?

____

NAME ________________________

Lesson 6.2 Create a Bar Graph

You can use an electronic spreadsheet to create a bar graph or you can create it manually. Regardless of the method, the type of information you will provide for the graph is the same. Follow the steps below.

Phillips' Family Cars Miles Driven, April-Sept.			
Month	**Subcompact**	**Full-Size Sedan**	**Pickup Truck**
April	1,250	903	1,110
May	1,650	867	1,237
June	1,832	1,252	1,349
July	1,400	1,390	1,898
Aug.	1,280	1,367	1,278
Sept.	1,345	1,445	890

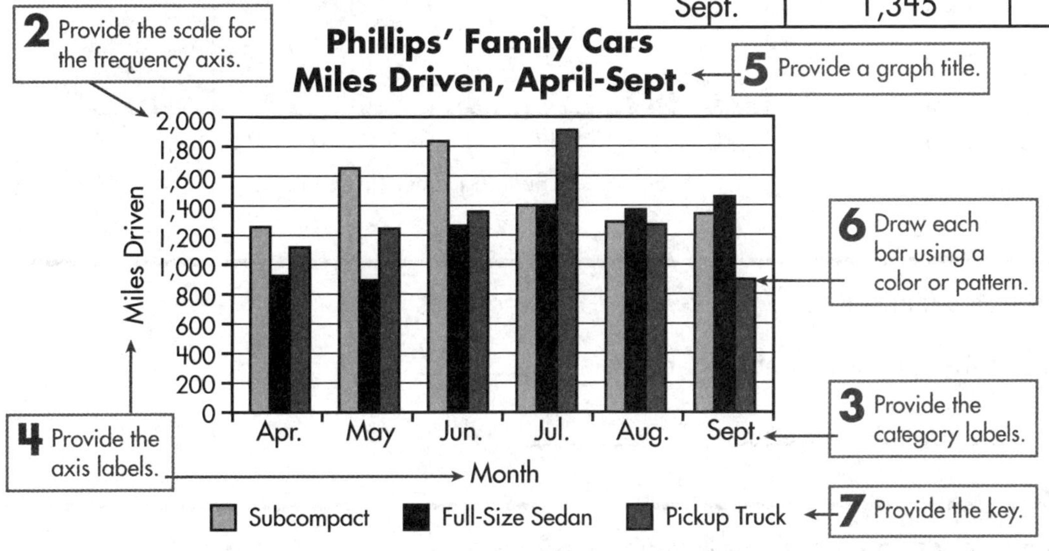

Create a multiple bar graph on a separate piece of paper using the information in the table. Then, refer to the table and your graph to answer the questions.

George Martin Sources of Income, 2007–2011			
Year	**Full-time Job**	**Invest-ments**	**Part-time Job**
2007	$22,745	$16,800	$5,222
2008	$23,288	$15,825	$5,005
2009	$24,366	$15,222	$4,789
2010	$25,456	$17,200	$2,200
2011	$28,972	$14,432	$1,200

1. What was George's total income in

   2007? ________ in 2011? ________

2. What was George's income from his full-time job in 2007? ________

   in 2011? ________

3. George's income from his full-time job increased steadily every year from 2007 to 2011. Why didn't his total income increase? ____________________

NAME ____________________

Lesson 6.3 Histograms

A **histogram** is a type of bar graph. In a histogram, the categories are consecutive and the intervals are equal. Each bar shows a range of data. There is no space between the bars.

A histogram is created from a **frequency table**, as shown below.

An interval that does not have a frequency does not have a bar.

100 Meter Dash	
Running Times	**Frequency**
10.5–11	1
11–11.5	0
11.5–12.0	6
12.0–12.5	4
12.5–13.0	5

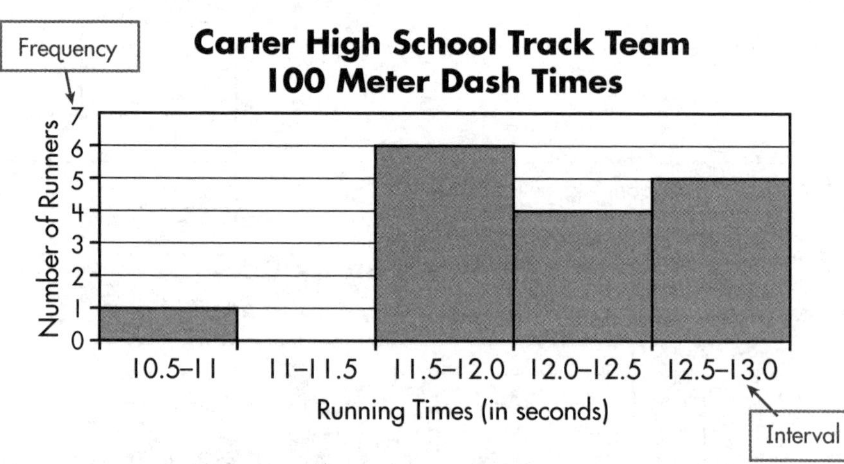

Refer to the table and histogram above to answer the following questions.

1. Which interval has the greatest number of runners? ________

2. Which interval does not have a frequency? ________

Refer to the histogram below to answer the following questions.

3. What information is shown on the frequency axis? ________

4. What do the intervals show? ________

5. How many employees drive 15 miles or less to work? ________

6. How many employees drive more than 15 miles to work? ________

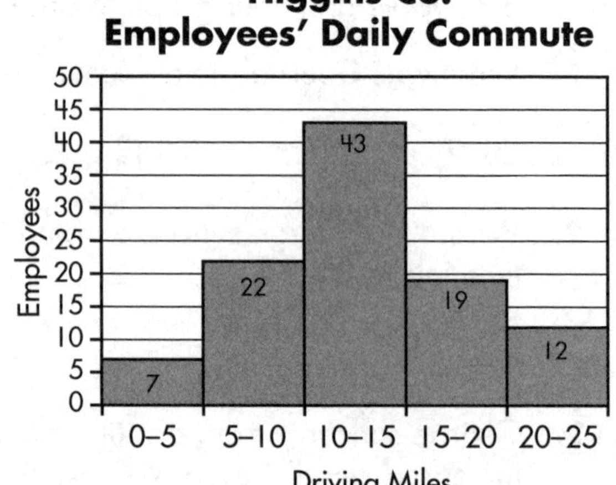

NAME ____________________

Lesson 6.4 Create a Histogram

Follow the steps below to create a histogram.

1. Data must be collected in a frequency table. List the data intervals (the Age Group column in the example below). Fill in the Frequency column.

Survey Respondents	
Age Group	Frequency
20–35	367
35–50	436
50–65	522
65–80	467
80–95	128

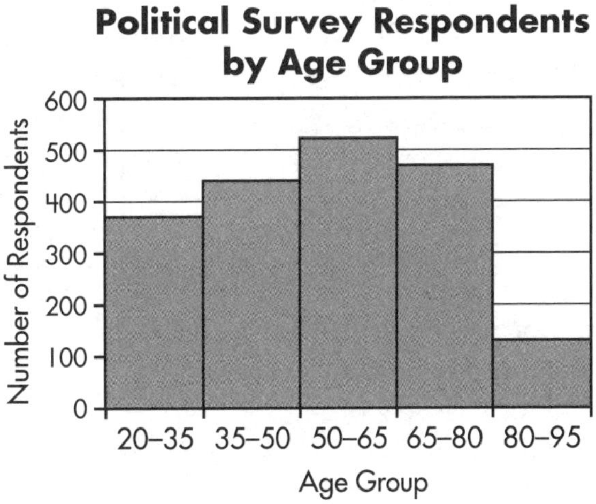

Political Survey Respondents by Age Group

2. Draw and label the vertical and horizontal axes in your histogram. Provide a graph title.
3. Put the intervals on the horizontal axis and the frequencies on the vertical axis.
4. Draw in the bars. The intervals should be equal, so there should be no space between the bars. An interval with a frequency of 0 will have no bar.

Leland Outdoor Products must have enough service representatives to answer the phones during peak periods. A manager tracked the average number of customer calls for 3 months and put them in the frequency table below. Create a histogram on a separate piece of paper, and answer the following questions.

1. What information should go on the horizontal axis of your histogram? ________

   the vertical axis? ________

2. The scale interval on the frequency axis would appear best in increments of: (circle one)

   25 50 100 500

3. The manager needs additional staff to handle more than 300 calls in a time period. During which time periods might the manager need to add additional staff?

   ____

Leland Outdoor Products	
Time Period	Average Number of Calls
8–10 am	172
10 am–12 pm	345
12–2 pm	290
2–4 pm	567
4–6 pm	580

NAME ____________________

Lesson 6.5 Line Graphs

A **line graph** shows how two variables relate to each other and how they change over time. The line graph at right shows the specific values at each data point.

A line graph shows data trends over time that may help you to make predictions. This could help to analyze or solve a problem. For example, Pelworth Technology School may need to look closely at enrollment data to adjust staffing for future enrollments.

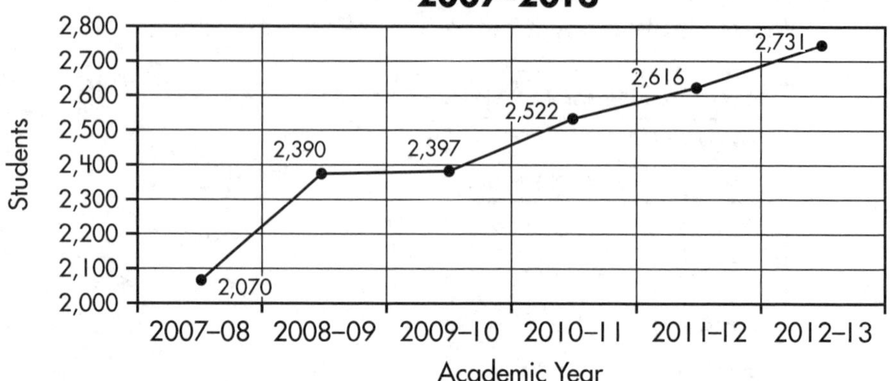

When analyzing data, you may need to calculate the percent of increase or decrease from one period to another. Remember that a percentage increase or decrease is in relation to the original value. Use the formula below:

$$\frac{\text{amount of increase or decrease}}{\text{original amount}} = \text{percent increase or decrease}$$

Refer to the line graph above to answer the following questions.

1. What information does the graph show during the time period? ____________________

2. What general trend does the graph show from the academic year

   2007–2008 to 2012–2013? ____________________

3. Which academic years do not follow this general trend? ____________________

4. Calculate the enrollment change from 2007–2008 to 2012–2013. Round your answer to the nearest whole percent.

   ____

5. Based on the percent of change you calculated in question 4, estimate the enrollment for the school in another 6 years.

   ____

NAME ____________________

Lesson 6.5 Line Graphs

A **multiple line graph** shows changes over a period of time in more than one category. This allows you to compare data.

For example, the line graph at right compares the sales of three different stores during the same period of time (January to June) of the current year.

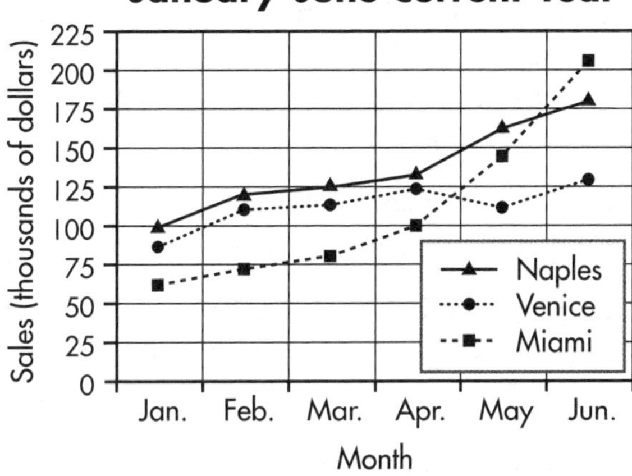

Refer to the graph above to answer the following questions.

1. Which store had the most consistent month-to-month sales? ________

2. Which store showed the greatest sales for a single month and the greatest overall change in sales from January to June? ________

Refer to the graph to answer the following questions.

3. In which weeks did each plant have the greatest growth?

   Plant A: ________

   Plant B: ________

   Plant C: ________

4. Which plant had greater growth each week than the week before from Week 2 to Week 5?

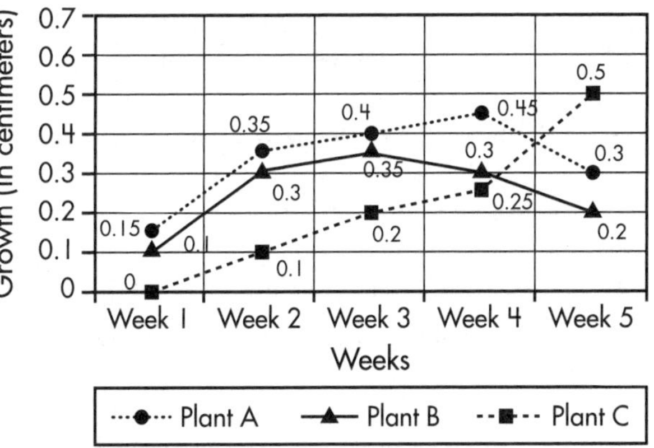

NAME ____________________

Lesson 6.6 Create a Line Graph

Follow the steps below to create a line graph.

1. Collect your data in a table as shown in the example at right. The table must include the time periods (intervals) during which the values will be measured.

2. Develop a scale for the values on the vertical axis; then, draw and label the vertical axis.

3. Draw and label the horizontal axis for the time periods. They are in months in the line graph to the right.

4. Provide a graph title and a title for each axis.

5. Plot the data on the graph by drawing a dot to show the value for each time period. Connect the dots with lines.

6. If you are creating a multiple bar graph like the one at the right, each set of lines and dots should relate to a key.

Kendra Parkinson Real Estate Single-Family Home Sales			
	2011	**2010**	**2009**
Jan.	432	210	110
Feb.	467	265	180
Mar.	420	385	175
April	776	540	165
May	723	589	203
June	769	540	208

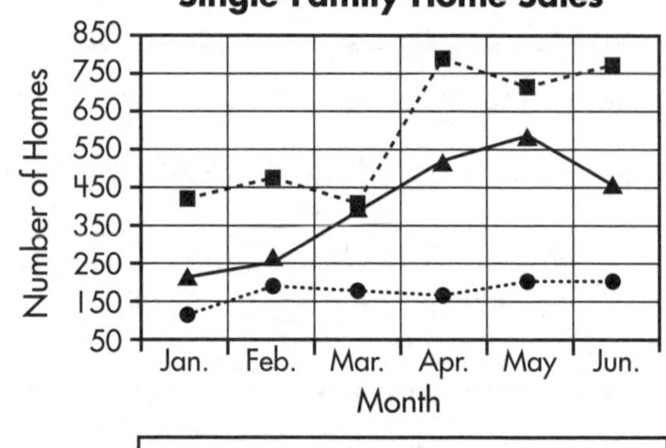

Create a multiple line graph on a separate piece of paper using the information in the table below. When you are finished, refer to the graph to answer the questions.

1. Which age group had the most subscriptions in 2007? ________

the fewest subscriptions? ________

2. In which year was there a decline in subscriptions in all four age groups?

____

3. Which two age groups show the greatest overall potential for growth in subscriptions in future years? ________ ________

Mountain Hiking Online Magazine Subscriptions 2007–2010				
Age Group	**2007**	**2008**	**2009**	**2010**
20–35	8,700	6,320	6,895	7,119
35–50	7,223	7,000	8,778	9,654
50–65	4,002	3,822	6,200	6,620
65–80	1,041	890	1118	1,297

NAME ______________________

Lesson 6.7 Circle Graphs

A circle graph is used to show parts of a whole. The entire circle represents 100%. The circle is divided into sectors, which are fractional parts of the whole. The table and figure below show how a percentage relates to a fraction and the degree measure of the sectors of a circle.

Sector	Percent	Fraction	Degree Measure
	100%	one whole	360°
A	50%	$\frac{1}{2}$	180°
B	25%	$\frac{1}{4}$	90°
C	12.5%	$\frac{1}{8}$	45°
D	6.25%	$\frac{1}{16}$	22.5°

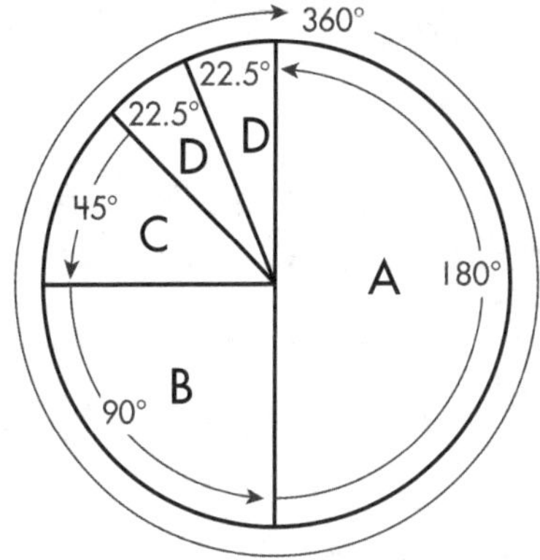

A circle graph can be divided into any number of sectors of any percentage/fraction value. The total will always be 100%, one whole, or 360°. For the circle above,

$180° + 90° + 45° + 22.5° + 22.5° = 360°$, or: $\frac{1}{2} + \frac{1}{4} + \frac{1}{8} + \frac{1}{16} + \frac{1}{16} = 1$

Determine the percentage and number of degrees for each segment. Use a protractor, if necessary.

1. Sector A ________ % or ________°

2. Sector B ________ % or ________°

3. Sector C ________ % or ________°

4. Sector D ________ % or ________°

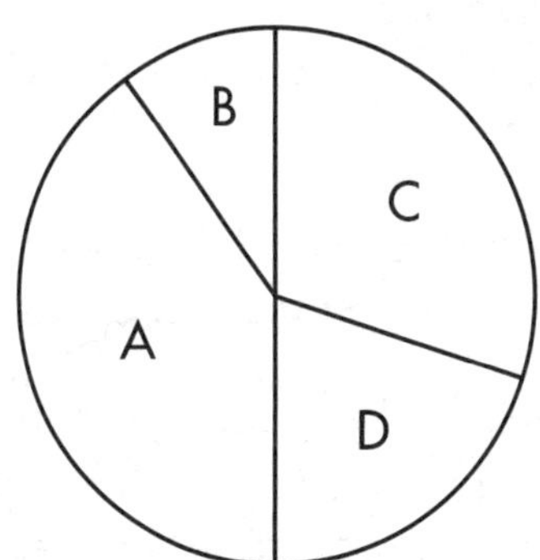

Draw the sectors in the table on the circle to the right. Use a protractor. Label each sector of the circle with the percentage and degree angle.

5.

Sectors
15%
25%
35%
15%
10%

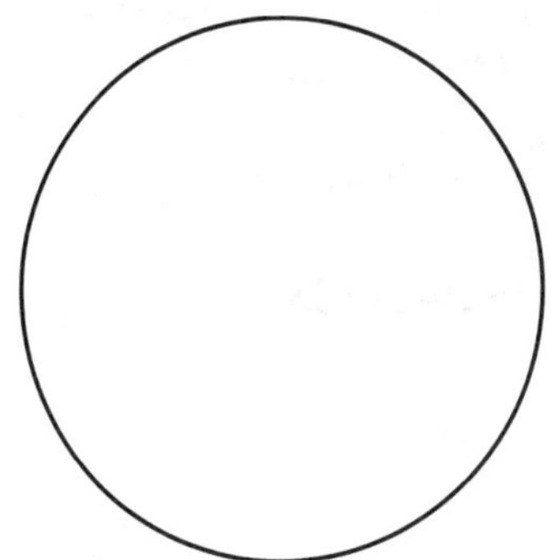

NAME ____________________

Lesson 6.7 Circle Graphs

A circle graph shows the relationship of each sector to the whole, or 100%.

What are Crawford County's total expenditures for the current year?

$13,573,452

Which category is the greatest portion of the Crawford County yearly expenses?

education

How much did Crawford County spend on insurance in the current year?

$1,044,984, or 8%

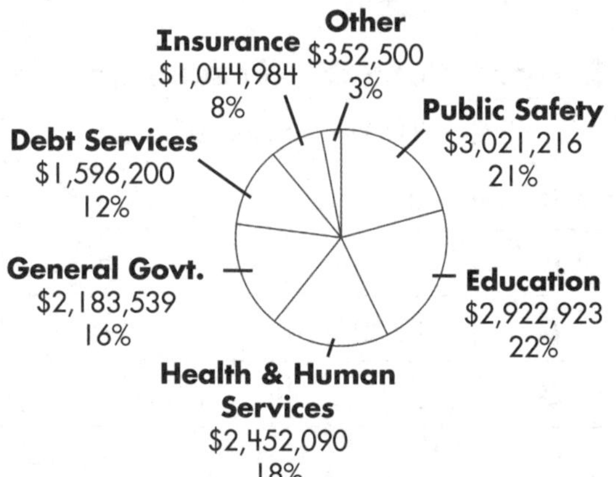

Refer to the circle graph and table to answer the following questions.

1. The circle graph and table at right are complete except for the percentages. Calculate the percentage for each income source and write it in the percent column in the table. Round percents to the nearest tenth.

2. What is Crawford County's greatest single source of income? ________

3. What total percentage of its income does Crawford County get from grants from the state and federal governments? ________

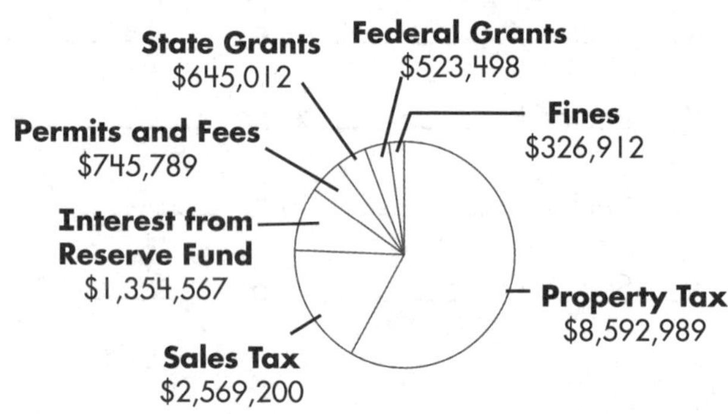

4. Compare the Crawford County Income graph to the graph at the top of this page. Did Crawford County have more income than expenses or more expenses than income? Record the difference on the correct line below.

   more income than expenses ________________

   more expenses than income ________________

Income Source	Percent
Property Tax	
Interest from Reserve Fund	
Sales Tax	
Permits and Fees	
Fines	
State Grants	
Federal Grants	

NAME ______________________________

Lesson 6.8 Create a Circle Graph

Follow the steps below to create a circle graph.

1. Organize the graph information in a table. See the example at right. If necessary, calculate each sector as a percent of the whole. The percentages in the graph to the right are rounded to the nearest whole percent.
2. Label each sector with a descriptive name and the percentage, or create a color-coded key. In the graph at right, the sector labels, values, and percentages have been included.
3. If you wish, add a distinctive color or pattern to each sector.
4. Add a graph title.

Wolton City Population by Age, 2011

Age Group	Number of People	Percent
Over 65	4,789	9%
45–64	13,200	24%
20–44	18,900	35%
5–19	12,100	22%
Under 5	5,400	10%

Wolton City
Population by Age Group, 2011

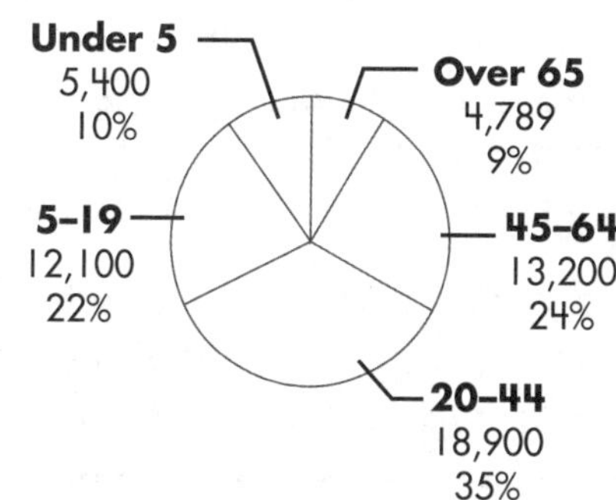

Follow the instructions below to create a pie graph. Then, answer the questions.

1. In the table at right, Kassie Lewis tracked the average number of weekday hours she spends doing various activities. Calculate the percents, rounding to the nearest tenth, and write them in the table. Then, create a circle graph on a separate piece of paper from the table data.
2. Kassie wants to find more time to spend with friends and family. About how many minutes is she spending now each day with friends and family?

   ____

3. Kassie is thinking of cutting back on her hobby and TV time. What percent of her day does she spend on hobbies and TV? ____________

Kassie Lewis Time Management

Activity	Average Hours per Day	Percent of 24-Hr. Day
Sleep	8.40	
Work	9.60	
Reading	0.72	
Errands & Housework	1.20	
Friends & Family	0.36	
Hobbies & TV	3.19	
Meals	0.53	

NAME ______________________

Lesson 6.9 Scatterplots

The data points in a scatterplot are plotted on a coordinate system as ordered pairs. (See Chapter 3 for more information on plotting ordered pairs.)

A **scatterplot** shows the relationship, or correlation, between two sets of data, or variables. The scatterplot to the right shows a positive correlation between weekly practice minutes on the *x*-axis and runs scored on the *y*-axis.

See the line drawn through the data points in the graph on the right. This **line of best fit** can help show the relationship between the two variables in the graph. The line of best fit is drawn so there are about an equal number of data points above and below the line.

What trend in the data is shown by the line of best fit? *As weekly practice minutes increase, the number of runs scored increases.*

Lorimer High Softball Team Weekly Practice and Runs Scored

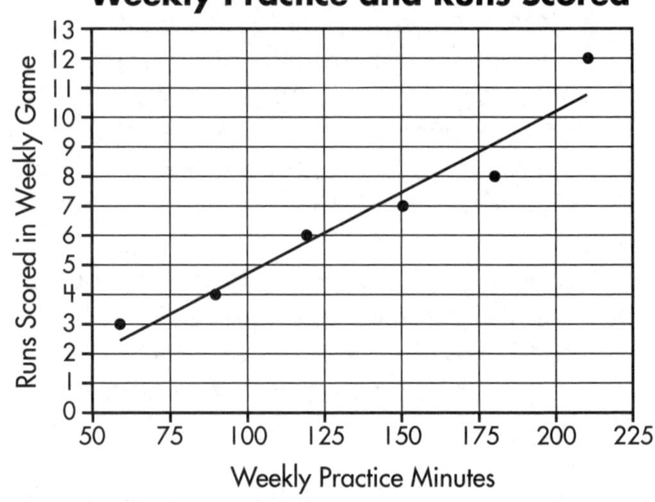

Weekly Practice Minutes	60	90	120	150	180	210
Runs Scored	3	4	6	7	8	12

Answer the questions by referring to the scatterplot.

Barker Real Estate Sales Agents and Units Sold

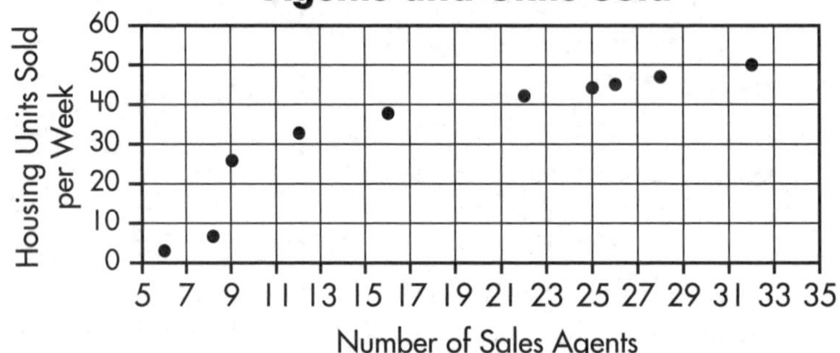

1. What two sets of data are being compared in the scatterplot?

____

2. Draw a line of best fit on the graph. What general trend does the graph show?

____

____

NAME ______________________________

Lesson 6.9 Scatterplots

When a line of best fit is drawn from the lower left to the upper right, there is a **positive correlation**. This means as *x* increases, *y* increases. The *x* and *y* variables have a stronger relationship the closer the data points are to the line. Data points in a perfectly straight line show the strongest relationship. A line of best fit may also help identify **outliers**, which are data points that do not conform to the general trend.

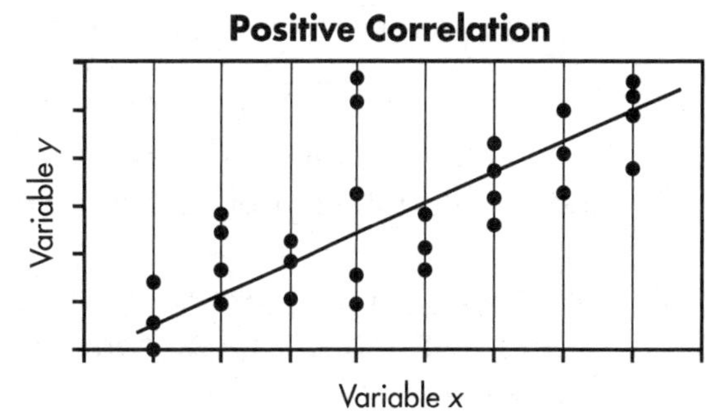

As variable *x* increases, *y* increases.

A line of best fit may run from the upper left to lower right (see figure at left below). In that case, the correlation is **negative**. Also, sometimes there is no correlation, as shown in the figure below on the right.

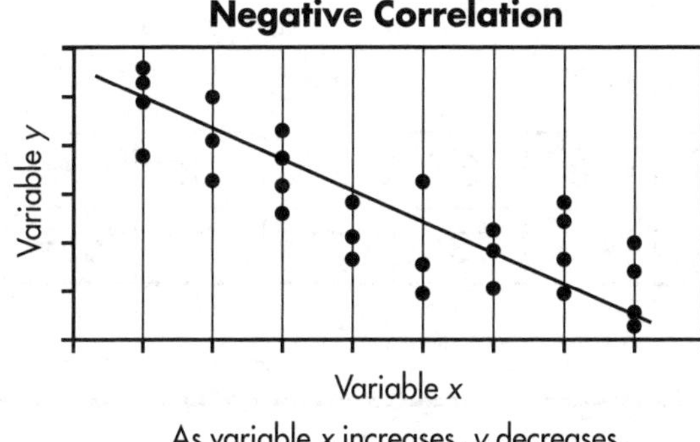

As variable *x* increases, *y* decreases.

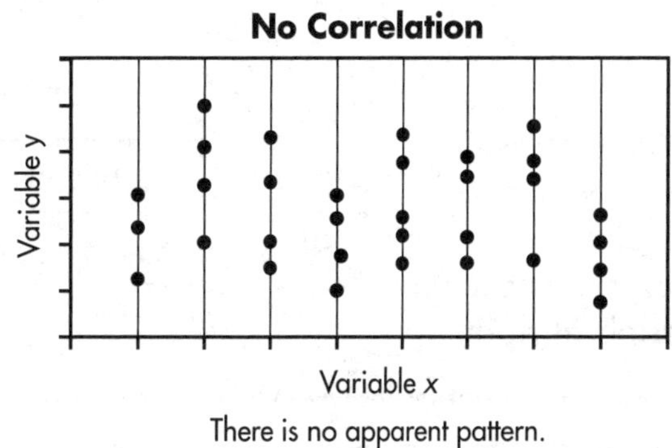

There is no apparent pattern.

Refer to the scatterplot below to answer the questions.

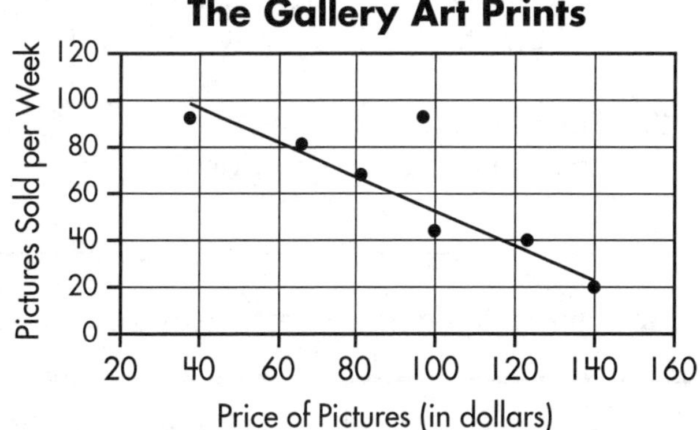

1. Explain the data point located at $98.

____

2. What type of correlation is shown by the graph data?

____

3. Predict the most likely result of lowering the prices of the pictures priced over $100.

____

NAME ______________________________

Lesson 6.10 Create a Scatterplot

Follow the steps below to create a scatterplot.

1. Organize your data in a table as shown in the example at right. The table will include the two variables you want to compare.

2. Develop a graph scale for the values on the *x*-axis (the horizontal axis) and the *y*-axis (the vertical axis).

3. Provide an overall graph title and a title for each axis.

4. Plot the data on the graph by drawing a dot for each value.

5. When analyzing the data, you may find it helpful to draw a line of best fit, as shown in the graph at right.

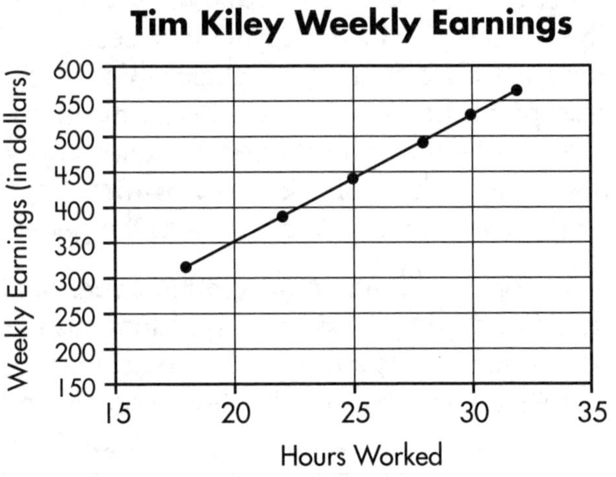

Tim Kiley Weekly Earnings

Hours Worked	18	22	25	28	30	32
Weekly Earnings	315	385	437.5	490	525	560

Follow the instructions below to create a scatterplot; then, answer the questions.

1. On a separate piece of paper, create a scatterplot from the data in the table. Draw a line of best fit.

Age	20	30	40	50	60	70
Minutes of Daily Exercise	110	108	72	64	44	20

2. Does the scatterplot show a correlation? If so, describe it.

____

3. Predict the number of minutes that an 80-year-old would exercise daily. ______________

On a separate piece of paper, create a scatterplot from the data in the table.

4. Does the scatterplot show a correlation? If so, describe it.

____

____

Carter High School Basketball Team									
Height (inches)	70	71	72	73	74	75	76	77	78
Average Points per Game	12	14	12	22	12	10	16	18	10

NAME ______________________

Lesson 6.11 Problem Solving

Solve each problem.

1. Wally's Sport Shop has its best sales in the summer months selling fishing equipment. In the table below, Wally recorded his summer sales data. For an overview, he would like to see it in a bar chart format. Create a bar chart on the blank graph below. Make sure to provide a scale for the frequency axis, category labels, axis labels, and a graph title. Also, draw in the bars.

	Sales Dollars (thousands)
April	26
May	45
June	65
July	72
Aug.	68
Sept.	55

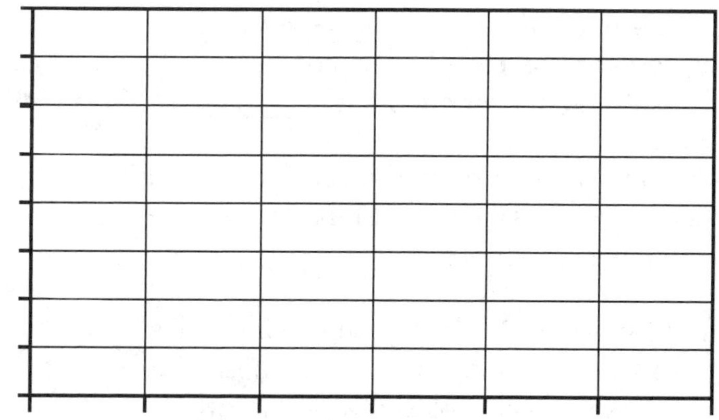

2. Refer to the graph you created in problem 1. In which month did sales peak and begin to decline? ____________

3. The East Side Softball League is made up of teams from four local communities that play teams in other towns. Answer the following questions about the graph below.

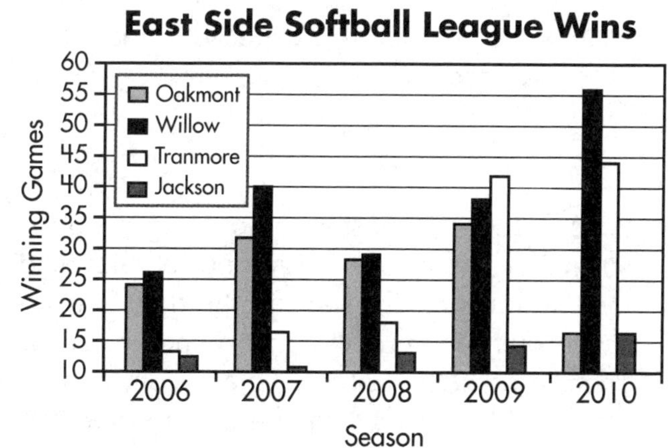

a. Which team had the poorest record from 2006 to 2010?

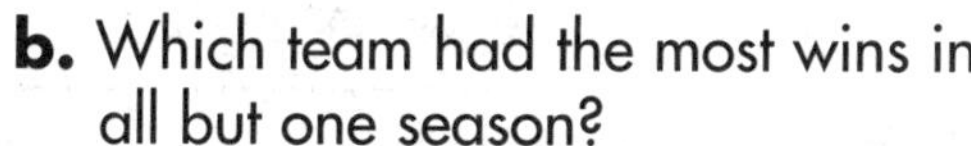

____

b. Which team had the most wins in all but one season?

____

c. Which team had more wins each year than the year before from 2007 to 2010?

____

d. How many more wins did Oakmont have in 2009 than in 2010? ____________

NAME ____________________

Lesson 6.11 Problem Solving

Solve each problem.

4. Mr. Alvarez wants to reduce his family's expenses. He put the family's expense data in the circle graph at right. Mr. Alvarez thinks that three categories of expenses could be reduced: cell phones, cars, and entertainment.

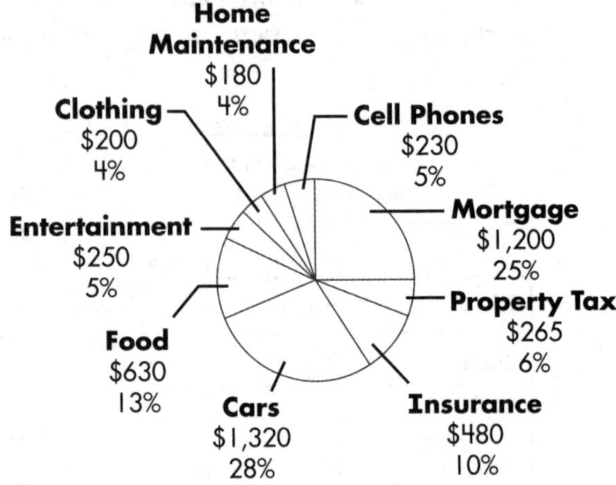

a. How much does the family spend altogether on cell phones, cars, and entertainment each month? ______

b. Cell phones, cars, and entertainment add up to what percentage of the family's monthly expenses? ______

5. Mr. Alvarez put his family on a budget. He tracked their total income and expenses for the next six months, as shown in the graph.

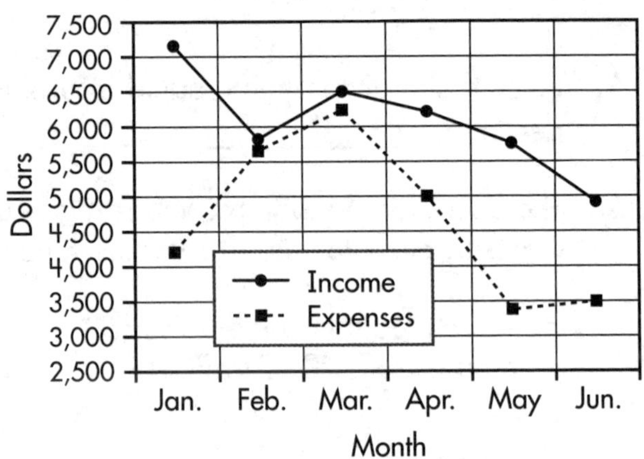

a. In which months did the family spend less than the average monthly expenses shown in the circle graph at the top of this page?

____

b. In which months did expenses almost equal income?

____

6. Pat's 2-pound trout stopped gaining weight, so she fed them a new fish food. She tracked their weights for five weeks. The data is in the scatterplot at the right. Draw a line of best fit. Then, predict the approximate weight of most of the fish if Pat feeds them the special food for a sixth week.

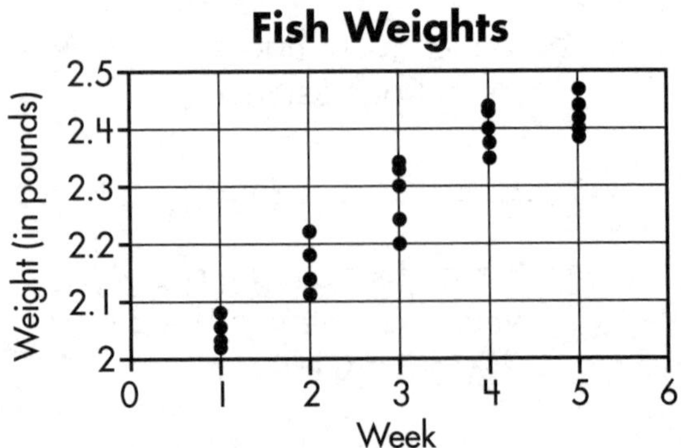

____

NAME ____________________

Check What You Learned

Creating and Interpreting Graphs

1. The sectors on the circle graph below were created from the data table. In the table, complete the percent and degrees columns. Round the percents and degrees to the nearest tenth. Then, complete the graph by including a graph title and sector labels. Match each item to the correct sector by measuring with a protractor, if necessary.

Tina's Gifts Annual Sales			
Item	**Sales**	**%**	**Degrees**
Music	$30,876		
Books	$22,245		
Jewelry	$37,890		
Cards	$4,200		
Clothing	$12,789		
Shoes	$16,740		
Perfume	$3,200		
Total:	**$127,940**		

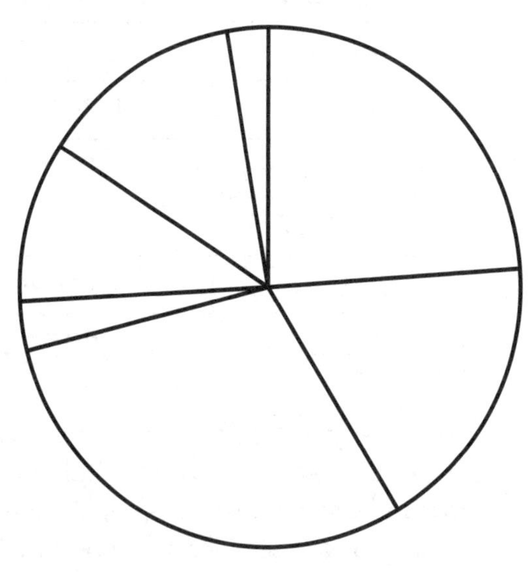

Refer to the multiple bar graph below to answer the following questions.

2. What does the graph show?

____

____

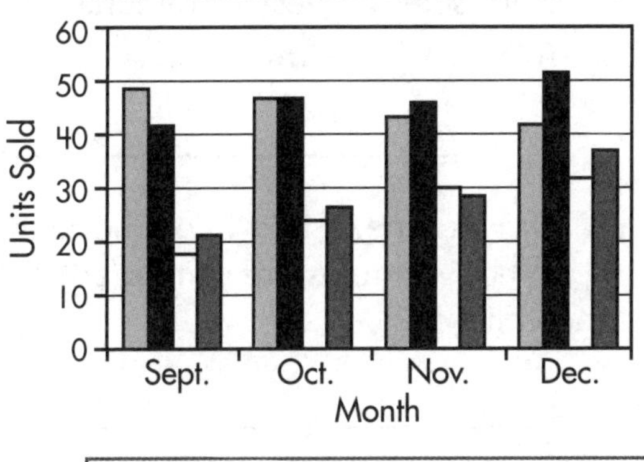

3. Which instruments had greater units sold each month than the month before from Oct. to Dec.?

____

4. Which instrument category showed the greatest one-month increase in units sold? __________

In which month did this increase occur? __________

5. In which month were sales greatest in total units sold? __________

CHAPTER 6 POSTTEST

NAME ______________________________

Check What You Learned

Creating and Interpreting Graphs

6. Before building a gas station at a new location, a manager did a traffic count to get an idea of the business volume. Using the blank graph, create a histogram from the data table.

Time Period	Number of Vehicles
6–8 am	372
8–10 am	1,795
10 am–12 pm	889
12–2 pm	1,567
2–4 pm	780
4–6 pm	1,495

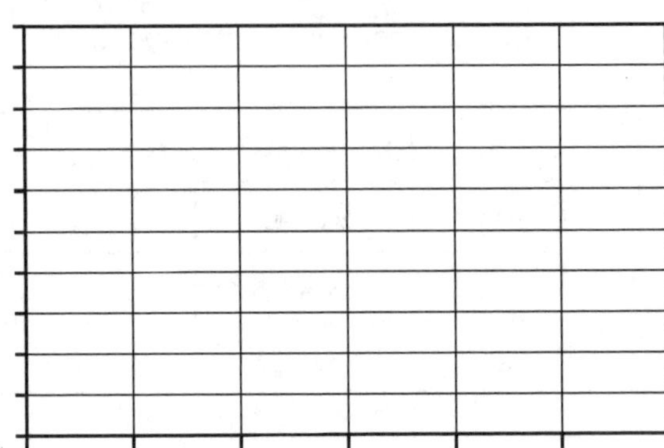

7. After her gas station was in operation, the manager made this multiple line graph based on sales data. Which grade of gas sold the most gallons for the day?

____

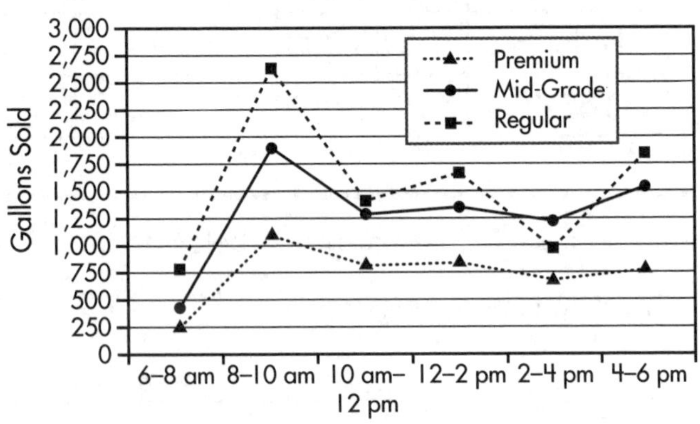

8. In the line graph, in which time period were sales highest for all three grades of gas?

____

9. Draw a line of best fit on the scatterplot. What variables are compared in the scatterplot?

____

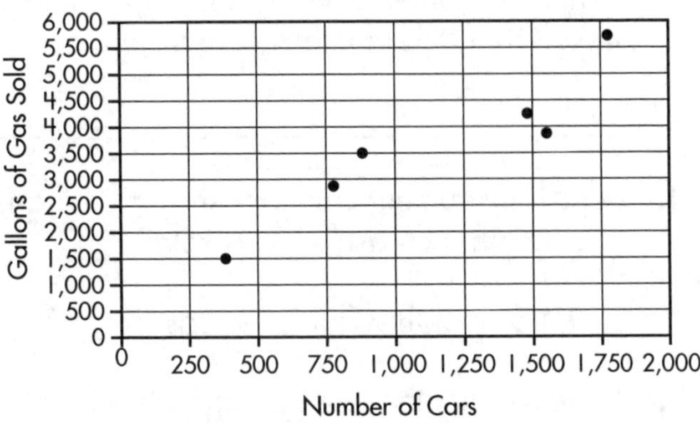

10. Does the scatterplot show a positive correlation, a negative correlation, or no correlation?

____

CHAPTER 6 POSTTEST

NAME ____________________

Final Test Chapters 1–6

Add, subtract, multiply, or divide. Write each answer in simplest form.

	a	b	c	d
1.	$2\frac{3}{16} + 1\frac{1}{32}$	$6\frac{7}{8} - 3\frac{1}{4}$	$\frac{2}{5} \times \frac{1}{12} =$	$6\frac{1}{2} \div 1\frac{3}{8} =$
2.	$4.66 + 2.18 + 0.02$	$8.33 - 4.12$	4.4×2.6	$1.5\overline{)27.45}$

Solve each problem.

3. Lita regularly walks $5\frac{1}{2}$ blocks during her lunch break. She is going to increase her pace so she walks $1\frac{2}{3}$ additional blocks. How many blocks will she walk during her lunch break?

Lita will walk __________ blocks during her lunch break.

4. Carson bought a new car for $32,460. Sales tax is 0.065 of the purchase price. How much sales tax will he pay?

Carson paid __________ in sales tax.

5. Morgan bought a boat for $7,500. Her payments are $340.90 per month. Her boat will be paid for in how many months?

Morgan's boat will be paid for in __________ months.

6. Tomás bought 3 toys for his collection. They cost $237.32, $67.87, and $44.28 plus tax which was 0.043 of the purchase price. How much did Tomás pay? Round up.

Tomás paid __________ for his toys.

NAME ______________________

Final Test Chapters 1–6

Underline the operation that should be done first. Then, find the value of the equation.

	a	b
7.	$15 \div (3 + 2) =$ ________	$(14 - 8) \times 2 + 4$ ________
8.	$18 - 8 \div 2 =$ ________	$[16 \div (4 - 2)] + 8$ ________

Name the property that each equation illustrates. The properties are commutative, associative, identity, or zero.

9.	$d \times (e \times f) = (d \times e) \times f$ ________	$1 \times w = w$ ________
10.	$n \times a = a \times n$ ________	$0 \div b = 0$ ________

Rewrite each expression using the distributive property.

11.	$(a - 2) \times 7 =$ ________	$k \times (m + n) =$ ________

Find the value of the variable in each equation.

	a	b	c
12.	$4 + x = 28$ ________	$52 + n = 188$ ________	$n - 86 = 72$ ________
13.	$19 + x = 55$ ________	$28 - x = 13$ ________	$n + 90 = 184$ ________

Write an equation for each problem. Then, find the value of the variable.

14. Casey had 222 coins in his collection. He sold 46 of the coins. How many coins are in his collection now?

________________ Casey has ________ coins.

15. A costume rental company had 158 costumes on Halloween morning. By the end of the day, 16 customers had picked up 3 costumes each. How many costumes did the rental company have left?

________________ The rental company had ________ costumes.

NAME ______________________

Final Test Chapters 1–6

Find the unknown number in each proportion.

	a	b	c
16.	$\frac{5}{30} = \frac{n}{12}$ ________	$\frac{n}{48} = \frac{12}{18}$ ________	$\frac{16}{24} = \frac{n}{96}$ ________
17.	$\frac{n}{56} = \frac{5}{8}$ ________	$\frac{4}{52} = \frac{8}{n}$ ________	$\frac{22}{n} = \frac{4}{8}$ ________

Plot each ordered pair on the grid.

18. $A\,(7, 7)$ $B\,(-5, 4)$

19. $C\,(-3, -2)$ $D\,(8, -2)$

20. $E\,(4, 3)$ $F\,(-6, -7)$

21. $G\,(5, -8)$ $H\,(-3, 3)$

22. $I\,(-6, 8)$ $J\,(5, 6)$

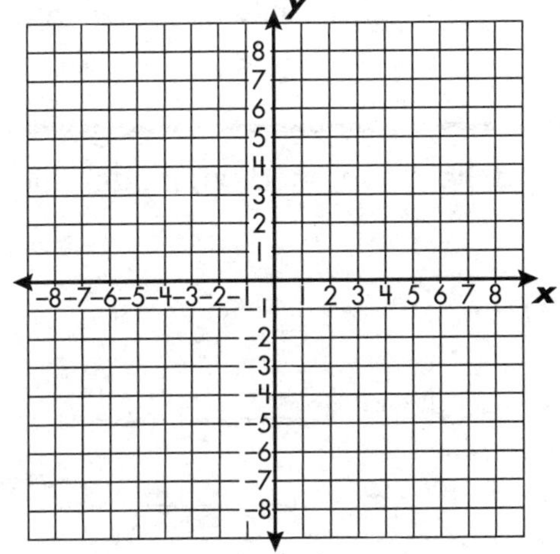

Solve the problems based on one spin of the spinner. Express each probability as a fraction in simplest form.

23. The number of possible outcomes is ______.

24. The probability of stopping on 8 is ______.

25. The probability of stopping on a letter is ______.

26. The probability of stopping on a number is ______.

27. The probability of stopping on a vowel is ______.

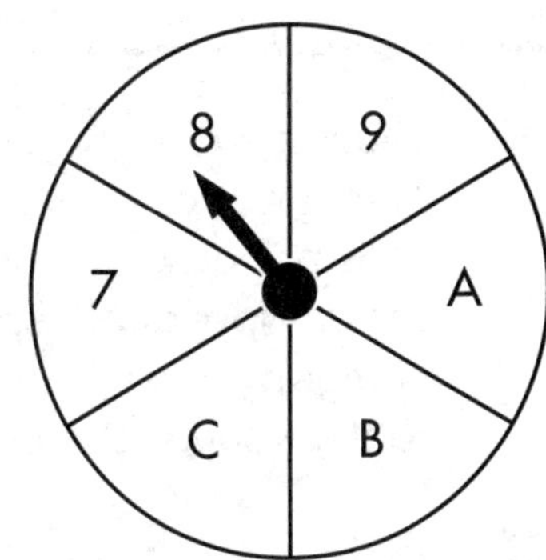

Solve the problem. Express probability as a fraction in simplest form.

28. Events Y and Z are mutually exclusive. $P(Y) = \frac{5}{8}$. $P(Z)$ is $\frac{1}{16}$. What is the probability that either Y or Z will occur?

P(Y) or P(Z) is ________

NAME ______________________

Final Test Chapters 1–6

Solve each problem. Express probabilities as fractions in simplest form.

29. Events C and D are independent. The probability that C will occur is $\frac{1}{3}$. The probability that D will occur is $\frac{1}{4}$. What is the probability that both C and D will occur?

The probability that both C and D will occur is __________

30. A bag contains 10 white toys and 12 green toys. What is the probability of choosing a white toy and then a green toy? (After choosing it, you would not replace the white toy.)

The probability of choosing a white toy and then a green toy is __________

Find the mean, median, mode, and range of each set of data. Round to the nearest tenth.

31.

	a	b	c
	8, 12, 8, 7, 11	32, 15, 18, 14, 30, 27	5, 7, 2, 13, 11, 17, 14, 13
mean:	__________	__________	__________
median:	__________	__________	__________
mode:	__________	__________	__________
range:	__________	__________	__________

32. The table at right shows the number of customer service calls per day for a year for an appliance repair company. Complete the table. Round to tenths.

33. How many days did the company get between 150–199 calls?

____

Customer Service Calls			
Number of Calls	**Frequency (Days)**	**Cumulative Frequency**	**Relative Frequency**
0–49	16		%
50–99	48		%
100–149	57		%
150–199	60		%
200–250	46		%

34. What percentage of days did the company get between 0–49 calls? __________

NAME ____________________

Final Test Chapters 1–6

Use the line plot to answer the questions.

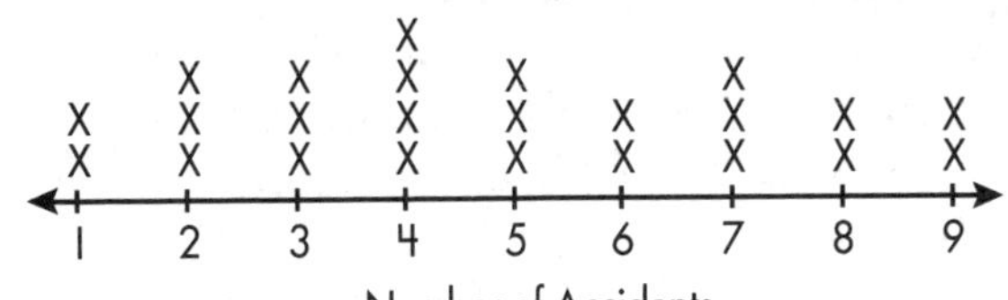

35. What is the mode? ________

36. What is the range? ________

37. What is the median? ________

38. How many months does the plot include? ________

Refer to the circle graph to answer the questions.

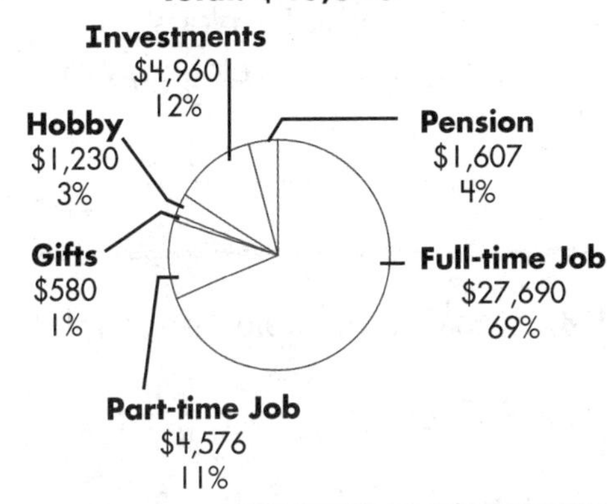

39. What does the graph show?

____

40. What is Jan's greatest source of income?

____

Refer to the line graph to answer the questions.

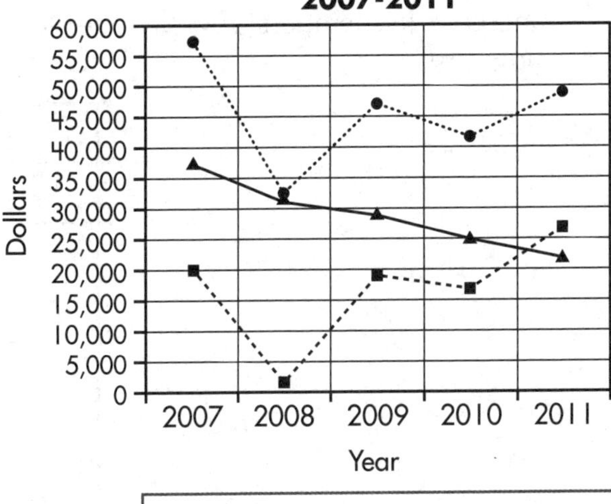

41. What does the graph show? ________

____

42. In which year did expenses equal income?

____

43. In which year were savings greater than expenses?

____

44. In which years did expenses decline from the previous year?

____

NAME ______________________

Final Test Chapters 1–6

Biologists were concerned about the declining population of a rare lizard, so they restricted human access to the lizard breeding area. The biologists then collected population data for 6 years. Refer to the scatterplot to answer the questions.

45. In which year did limiting human access to the area begin to affect the lizard population?

____

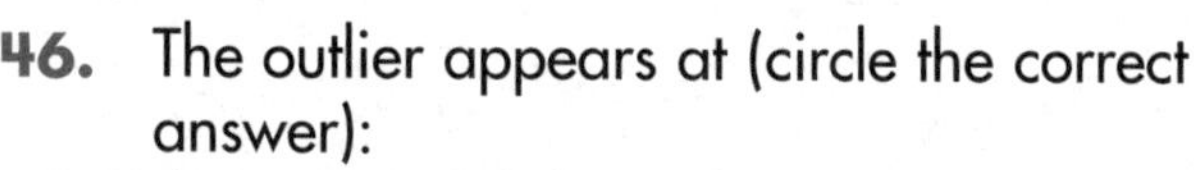

46. The outlier appears at (circle the correct answer):

(0, 400)   (6, 650)   (5, 300)

47. Does the scatterplot show a positive correlation, a negative correlation, or no correlation?

____

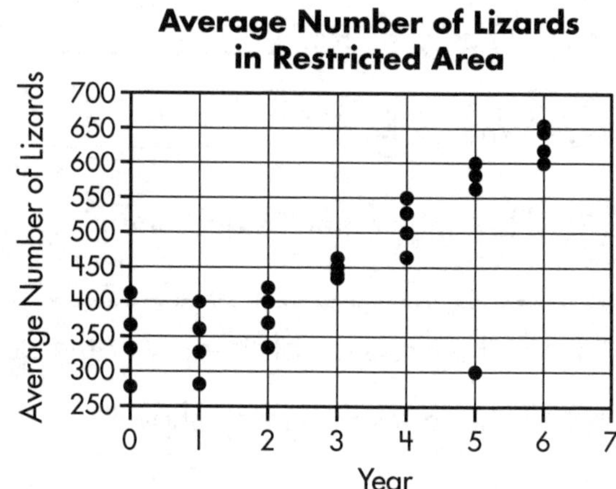

48. Make a multiple bar graph below from the data table, and then answer the questions.

49. Which age group has the greatest number of members? ________

the fewest number? ________

50. Which age group shows the greatest increase in members from October to January?

____

Westside Health Club Membership				
Age Group	**Oct.**	**Nov.**	**Dec.**	**Jan.**
20–35	625	635	698	743
35–50	722	702	726	793
50–65	422	435	470	544

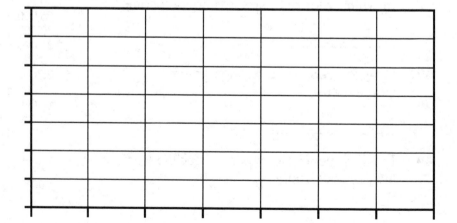

NAME ______________________ DATE ____________

Scoring Record for Posttests, Mid-Test, and Final Test

		Performance			
Chapter Posttest	Your Score	Excellent	Very Good	Fair	Needs Improvement
1	____ of 10	10	8–9	6–7	5 or fewer
2	____ of 16	15–16	13–14	11–12	10 or fewer
3	____ of 14	14	12–13	10–11	9 or fewer
4	____ of 16	15–16	13–14	11–12	10 or fewer
5	____ of 16	15–16	13–14	11–12	10 or fewer
6	____ of 10	10	8–9	6–7	5 or fewer
Mid-Test	____ of 35	33–35	29–32	22–28	21 or fewer
Final Test	____ of 50	46–50	41–45	35–40	34 or fewer

Record your test score in the Your Score column. See where your score falls in the Performance columns. Your score is based on the total number of required responses. If your score is fair or needs improvement, review the chapter material.

Data Analysis and Probability Answers

Chapter 1

Check What You Know, page 1

	a	b	c	d
1.	$1\frac{1}{4}$	$4\frac{4}{15}$	$2\frac{1}{6}$	$1\frac{11}{12}$
2.	$\frac{1}{4}$	$6\frac{2}{5}$	$\frac{3}{8}$	3
3.	6.1	8.675	1.83	3.744
4.	25.5	0.946	0.0056	9.4149
5.	1.6	500	41.3	5.586

Check What You Know, page 2

6. 49 gal.
7. 5; $\frac{11}{12}$
8. \$15.81; \$4.19
9. 27.15
10. 4.12

Lesson 1.1, page 3

1. 1, 5
   1, 2, 3, 5, 6, 10, 15, 30
   1, 5; 5
2. 1, 2, 5, 10
   1, 2, 4, 5, 10, 20
   1, 2, 5, 10; 10
3. 1, 2, 3, 4, 6, 12
   1, 2, 3, 6, 9, 18
   1, 2, 3, 6; 6

	a	b	c
4.	$\frac{1}{6}$	$\frac{1}{2}$	$\frac{5}{6}$
5.	$3\frac{2}{3}$	$4\frac{3}{4}$	$5\frac{1}{4}$

Lesson 1.2, page 4

	a	b
1.	$\frac{4}{12}$ and $\frac{3}{12}$	$\frac{24}{40}$ and $\frac{15}{40}$
2.	$\frac{4}{8}$ and $\frac{7}{8}$	$\frac{3}{18}$ and $\frac{2}{18}$
3.	$\frac{15}{20}$ and $\frac{2}{20}$	$\frac{4}{6}$ and $\frac{1}{6}$
4.	$\frac{8}{56}$ and $\frac{21}{56}$	$\frac{5}{10}$ and $\frac{6}{10}$
5.	$\frac{3}{16}$ and $\frac{4}{16}$	$\frac{9}{24}$ and $\frac{4}{24}$

Lesson 1.3 page 5

	a	b	c	d
1.	$\frac{19}{8}$	$\frac{4}{1}$	$\frac{27}{8}$	$\frac{3}{2}$
2.	$\frac{16}{3}$	$\frac{11}{5}$	$\frac{13}{8}$	$\frac{23}{1}$
3.	$\frac{38}{5}$	$\frac{8}{3}$	$\frac{7}{3}$	$\frac{35}{4}$
4.	$2\frac{1}{8}$	$4\frac{1}{9}$	4	$3\frac{1}{2}$
5.	$7\frac{2}{5}$	$1\frac{2}{13}$	$2\frac{1}{4}$	10
6.	$3\frac{1}{6}$	$12\frac{1}{2}$	$1\frac{5}{7}$	$1\frac{1}{3}$

Lesson 1.4, page 6

	a	b	c	d
1.	$\frac{8}{15}$	$\frac{2}{3}$	$\frac{7}{24}$	$\frac{1}{12}$
2.	$6\frac{1}{8}$	$4\frac{3}{8}$	$\frac{5}{24}$	$2\frac{9}{10}$

3. $7\frac{1}{9}$ lb.
4. $11\frac{5}{12}$ lb.

Lesson 1.5, page 7

	a	b	c	d
1.	$\frac{3}{14}$	$\frac{5}{8}$	$\frac{1}{18}$	$\frac{1}{25}$
2.	$\frac{1}{8}$	$\frac{3}{8}$	10	$\frac{9}{16}$

3. $\frac{3}{8}$ c. butter, $\frac{3}{4}$ c. sugar, $1\frac{9}{16}$ c. flour, $1\frac{1}{8}$ tsp. ginger
4. $2\frac{1}{2}$ c. butter, 5 c. sugar, $10\frac{5}{12}$ c. flour, $7\frac{1}{2}$ tsp. ginger

Lesson 1.6, page 8

	a	b	c	d
1.	$\frac{7}{3}$	$\frac{5}{6}$	$\frac{1}{29}$	$\frac{9}{20}$
2.	$1\frac{1}{2}$	2	$6\frac{1}{4}$	$1\frac{11}{12}$
3.	$2\frac{12}{13}$	8	$5\frac{1}{3}$	$\frac{9}{20}$
4.	$\frac{5}{6}$	$\frac{1}{2}$	$\frac{15}{22}$	66

5. $12\frac{1}{2}$ mpg

Lesson 1.7, page 9

	a	b	c
1.	0.5	1.75	0.060
2.	3.4	2.15	5.075
3.	4.2	5.90	4.328
4.	2.8390	1.1920	3.8184
5.	$\frac{9}{10}$	$3\frac{1}{2}$	$4\frac{4}{5}$
6.	$\frac{1}{4}$	$2\frac{9}{20}$	$6\frac{11}{100}$
7.	$\frac{41}{200}$	$1\frac{111}{125}$	$2\frac{41}{200}$

Lesson 1.8, page 10

	a	b	c	d	e
1.	1.1	8.3	41.79	8.295	1.3202
2.	6.075	1.9043	14.0261	20.246	6.6157
3.	0.2	1.98	13.87	1.939	31.711

4. 60.20
5. 7.03

Lesson 1.9, page 11

	a	b	c	d	e
1.	8.2	1.05	23.210	435.5	50.05
2.	120.24	13.272	1.008	3.0173	1.3612
3.	15.043	0.01220	0.00018	3.10486	1.11456

4. \$16.95
5. \$305.64

Lesson 1.10, page 12

	a	b	c	d
1.	0.4	0.45	0.602	0.0206
2.	80	120	7,100	6,000
3.	24.5	0.32	31,000	1.6

Lesson 1.11 page 14

Step 5. Interpretations will vary, but they should answer the original question, including a comparison between males and females. Example: Dogs are the most popular pet overall, but males prefer dogs more strongly than females do.

Data Analysis and Probability Answers

Check What You Learned, page 15

	a	b	c	d
1.	$3\frac{1}{24}$	$5\frac{1}{15}$	$\frac{2}{3}$	$\frac{2}{9}$
2.	$\frac{1}{8}$	16	$9\frac{1}{3}$	$\frac{3}{4}$
3.	5.64	2.936	1.524	0.195
4.	29.24	7.176	4.5402	2.54868
5.	25.3	35	2.08	291.8

Check What You Learned, page 16

6. $11\frac{3}{4}$
7. $16\frac{1}{2}$
8. 37.962 km
9. $52.70
10. 8.3

Chapter 2

Check What You Know, page 17

	a	b
1.	12; n	1; d
2.	$2 \times 3 < n$	$n \times 5$
3.	$8 - 5$; 5	$(4 + 2)$; 2
4.	$4 \div 2$; 8	$(5 - 3)$; 11
5.	commutative	zero
6.	identity	associative
7.	$(8 \times 3) + (8 \times 6)$	$n \times (5 - 2)$
8.	$6 \times (a + b)$	$(f \times 7) - (4 \times 7)$

Check What You Know, page 18

	a	b	c
9.	5	10	5
10.	84	81	3
11.	22	4	48

12. $6 \times n = 72$ or $72 \div 6 = n$; 12
13. 200
14. 100
15. 2007 and 2008
16. 2009 and 2010; The line rises most steeply between those 2 years.

Lesson 2.1, page 19

	a	b	c
1.	expression	equation	inequality
2.	inequality	expression	equation
3.	8; n	1; y	
4.	2; x	10; d	
5.	$5 - n = 2$	$n < 4$	
6.	$3 \times 5 > n$	$2n - 5$	

Lesson 2.2, page 20

	a	b
1.	$12 + 9$; 7	7×6; 14
2.	3×2; 2	$12 \div 4$; 5
3.	7×3; 14	$(5 + 4)$; 27
4.	$80 \div 10$; 18	$(10 + 8 + 2)$; 4
5.	4×2; 7.4	$(9 - 4)$; 2
6.	$15 \div 5$; 24	$(5 + 7)$; 3.75
7.	$(12 - 6)$; 27	$(12 - 6)$; 102

Lesson 2.3, page 21

	a	b
1.	commutative	identity
2.	associative	identity
3.	zero	commutative
4.	16	$7 + (t + 8)$
5.	0	$5r \times p$
6.	$(3x + y) + z$	$90x$
7.	0	$3xy \times (6y \times 9)$

Lesson 2.4, page 22

	a	b
1.	$(5 \times 4) - (5 \times 2)$	$(t \times r) + (t \times s)$
2.	$7 \times (8 + 9)$	$(6 \times 11) - (4 \times 11)$
3.	$5 \times (n + m)$	$(y \times 8) - (y \times 3) - (y \times n)$
4.	$(f \times z) + (g \times z) + (h \times z)$	$t \times (t - c)$
5.	6	3
6.	15	2
7.	8	5

Lesson 2.5, page 23

	a	b	c
1.	13	4	18
2.	0	15	17
3.	16	24	100

4. $30 - n = 7$; 23
5. $108.50 + n = $219.99; $111.49

Lesson 2.6, page 24

	a	b	c
1.	5	4	56
2.	4	11	27
3.	25	80	3

4. $27 = 3 \times n$ or $27 \div 3 = n$; 9
5. $168 \div n = 12$ or $168 \div 12 = n$; 14

Lesson 2.7, page 25

1. 73°F; 21°F
2. 21°F + n = 73°F; 52

Data Analysis and Probability Answers

Lesson 2.7, page 26

3.

Average Temperatures in Tampa, FL	
Month	**Temperature**
January	60°F
February	62°F
March	67°F
April	71°F
May	77°F
June	81°F
July	83°F
August	82°F
September	81°F
October	75°F
November	68°F
December	62°F

4. 83°F; 60°F
5. 60°F + n = 83°F; 23
6. Chicago; Chicago's graph line is steeper than Tampa's line.

Check What You Learned, page 27

	a	b
1.	15; y	4; c
2.	33 + n × 6	n – 4 < 8
3.	2 × 5; 2	18 ÷ 6; 6
4.	(2 + 10); 2	(10 – 5); 5
5.	0	(4a × 3b) × c
6.	6g	17s + 9r
7.	(9 × 8) + (9 × m)	8 × (q – r)
8.	y × (13 + 7)	5q + 4q + 3q

Check What You Learned, page 28

	a	b	c
9.	39	77	12
10.	154	3	97
11.	37	16	5

12. 8 + 10 + n = 35; 17
13. 165 cm
14. 10 cm
15. 5 cm
16. slower; The graph line gets less steep as age increases.

Chapter 3

Check What You Know, page 29

	a	b	c
1.	3	5	8
2.	2	27	24
3.	<	>	>
4.	<	>	>
5.	8	–12	–6
6.	–2	451	–45

7. $\frac{75}{300} = \frac{120}{n}$ $n = 480$
8. $\frac{3,600}{30,000} = \frac{5,400}{n}$ $n = 45,000$

Check What You Know, page 30

9. 1,200; 1,200
10. 600
11. $\frac{380}{600}$; 63.3%
12. 293; 48.8%

13-15.

Grid 1

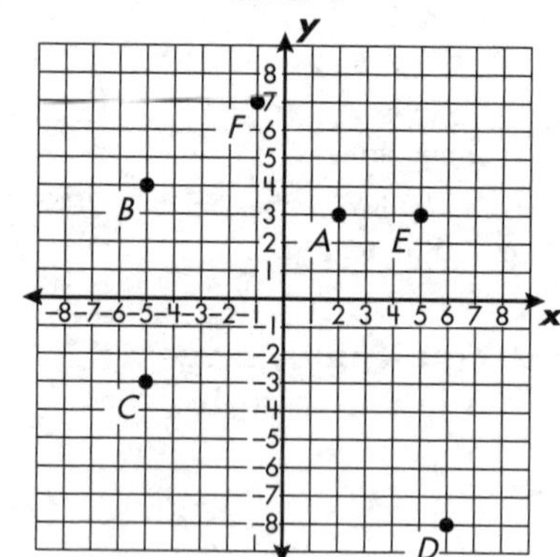

16. G (4, –4); H (7, 2)
17. I (–3, –5); J (–8, 7)
18. K (6, 7); L (–7, –5)

Lesson 3.1, page 31

	a	b	c
1.	True		
2.	True	True	
3.	True		
4.	True	True	
5.	True		True
6.		True	True
7.		True	

Lesson 3.1, page 32

	a	b	c
1.	24	10	1
2.	3	36	63
3.	60	5	2

4. $\frac{4,400}{18,612} = \frac{n}{20,000}$ n = 4,728 lbs.
5. $\frac{4.20}{100} = \frac{n}{4,000}$ n = $168

Data Analysis and Probability Answers

Lesson 3.2, page 33

	a	b	c
1.	3	96	2
2.	32	9	1
3.	80	1	11
4.	$\frac{20}{400} = \frac{n}{220}$	$20 \times 220 = 400 \times n$	$n = 11$
5.	$\frac{2}{6} = \frac{n}{48}$	$2 \times 48 = 6 \times n$	$n = 16$

Lesson 3.2, page 34

1. a. The group walks at 3 miles per hour: 82.5 miles/27.5 hours = 3/1, or 3 miles per hour
b. Miles left to walk: 150 – 82.5 = 67.5
c. The group should complete the walk on time: The group plans to walk 8 x 3 = 24 hours more. $\frac{3}{1} = \frac{n}{24}$ $n = 72$ miles they can walk in 24 hours

2. $\frac{1}{50} = \frac{n}{20{,}400}$ $n = 408$
3. $\frac{0.25}{1} = \frac{n}{21}$ $n = 5.25$ hrs.
4. $\frac{600}{8} = \frac{450}{n}$ $n = 6$ hrs.

Lesson 3.3, page 35

1. 615:1,185 615 ÷ 1,185 = 52%
2. $\frac{4}{5} = \frac{n}{365}$ 292 boxes

Lesson 3.3, page 36

1. $\frac{1}{3} = \frac{5}{n}$ $n = 15$ lb. x \$6.46 = \$96.90
2. middle school: $\frac{750 \text{ boys}}{600 \text{ girls}} = \frac{5}{4}$; high school: $\frac{1500 \text{ boys}}{1875 \text{ girls}} = \frac{4}{5}$
3. $\frac{44 \text{ hr.}}{7 \text{ mo.}} = \frac{n \text{ hr.}}{12 \text{ mo.}}$ $n = 75$ hr.
4. $\frac{1200}{1500} = \frac{4}{5}$ or 80%; No
5. $\frac{30 \text{ games}}{660 \text{ points}} = \frac{120 \text{ games}}{n}$ $n = 2{,}640$ points; no

Lesson 3.4, page 37

	a	b	c
1.	9	1	–10
2.	5	–4	–6
3.	<	<	>
4.	<	>	>

	a	b
5.	–10, –3, 0	9, 4, –1
6.	–10, –8, –3	–2, –5, –8

Lesson 3.5, page 38

	a	b	c
1.	11	1	–9
2.	–3	–9	0
3.	14	–8	–6
4.	–6	–4	–1
5.	8	3	–5
6.	–11	13	0

Lesson 3.6, page 39

	a	b	c
1.	36	–8	–2
2.	–4	3	–98
3.	–6	30	–11
4.	–4	6	70
5.	–196	–13	24
6.	–14	196	4
7.	20	–240	–2

Lesson 3.7, page 40

1-5.

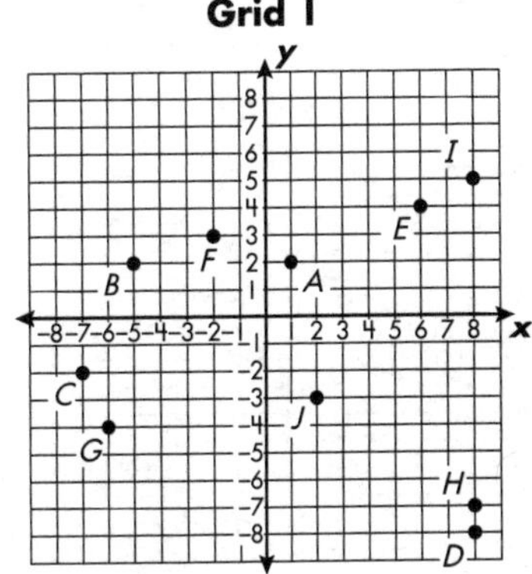

6. A (3, 3); B (–4, 6)
7. C (–5, –2); D (6, –3)
8. E (–2, 4); F (2, 3)
9. G (–5, –6); H (7, –7)
10. I (8, 5); J (–2, –3)

Lesson 3.7, page 41

1-5.

Grid 1

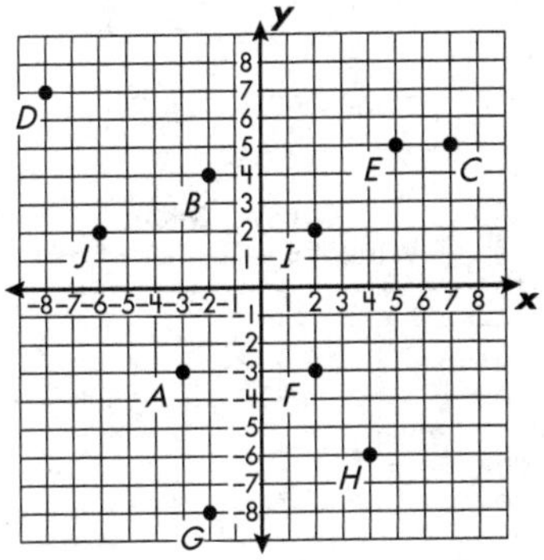

6. a. Quadrant I
   b. Quadrants II and III

Artifact	Coordinate
A	–5, 4
B	2, 2
C	–8, –7
D	4, 7
E	2, 4
F	–6, –5
G	7, –4
H	–4, –3
I	–7, 6
J	7, 4
K	3, –2
L	–4, 5

Grid 2

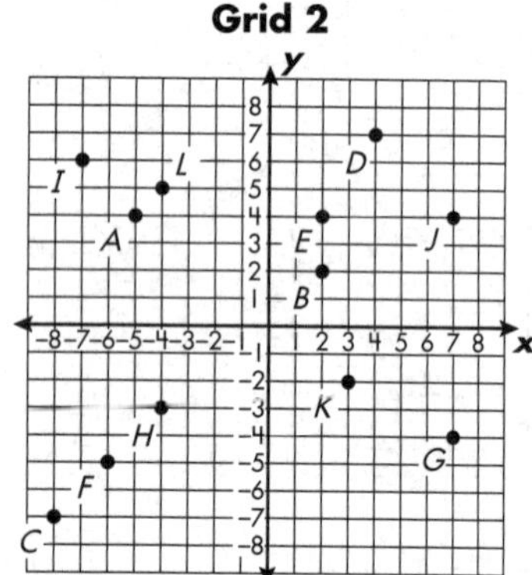

Lesson 3.8, page 42

1. $200

Boxes (x values)	Dollars (y values)
2	40
4	80
6	120
8	160

Carey's Roses Wholesale Cost per Box

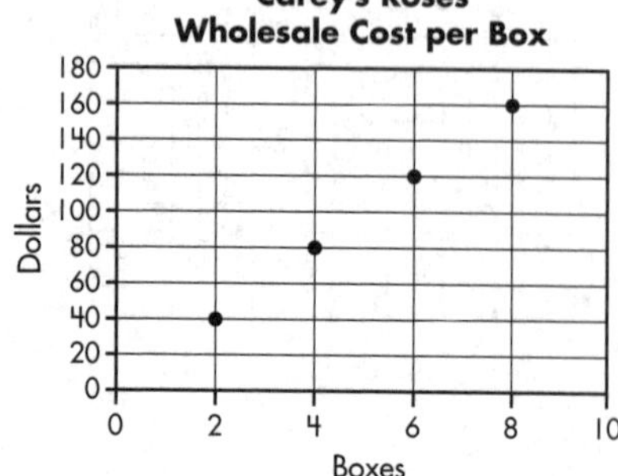

Lesson 3.8, page 43

1. Jack consistently used less gas than Bob did over the same distance.

Bob and Jack's Gas Use

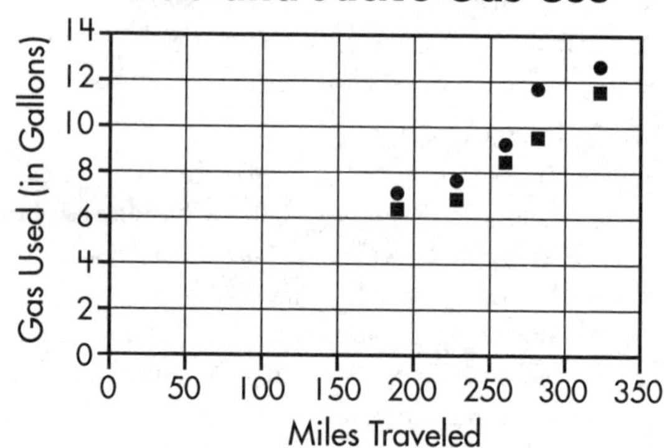

2. Grade increases as study hours increase.

Study Hours and Course Grade

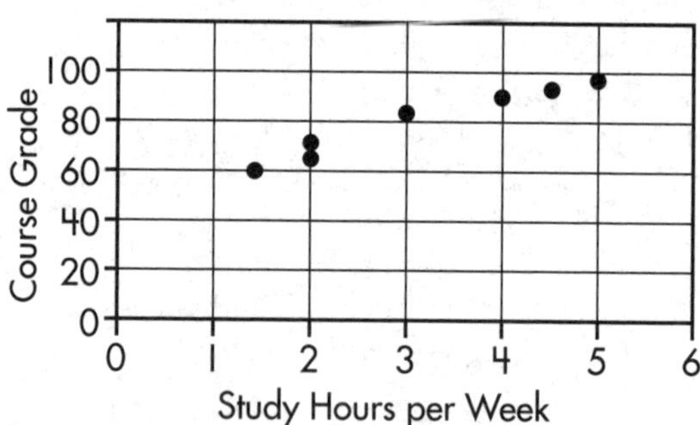

Lesson 3.9, page 44

Sunlight and Plant Growth

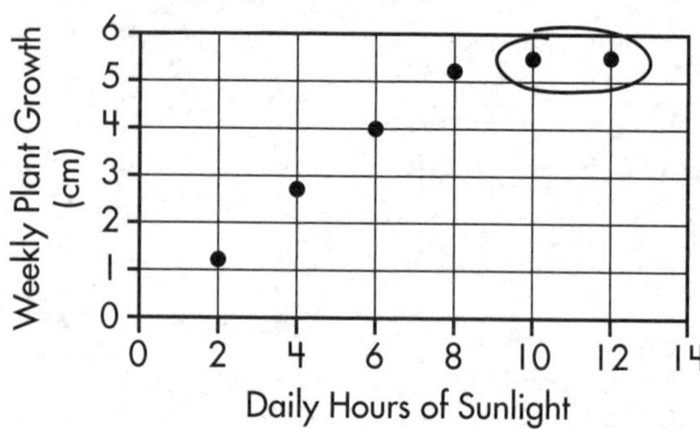

1. The more hours of sunlight, the greater the plant growth up to the point of 10 hours of sunlight.
2. a. Generally, the more hours he fished, the more fish he caught.
   b. Tuesday did not fit the pattern: only 2 fish in 4.5 hrs.

Data Analysis and Probability Answers

Fishing Results for One Week

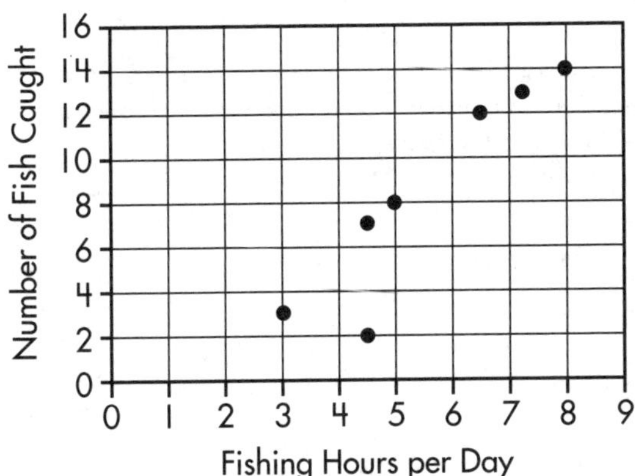

Check What You Learned, page 45

	a	b	c
1.	9	70	10
2.	2	18	28
3.	1	8	5
4.	–2	–11	35
5.	–2	7	3
6.	–405	–99	–6

7. $\frac{25}{4,500} = \frac{n}{27,000}$ $n = 150$

8. $\frac{80}{1,000} = \frac{n}{15,000}$ $n = \$1,200$

Check What You Learned, page 46

9-13.

Grid I

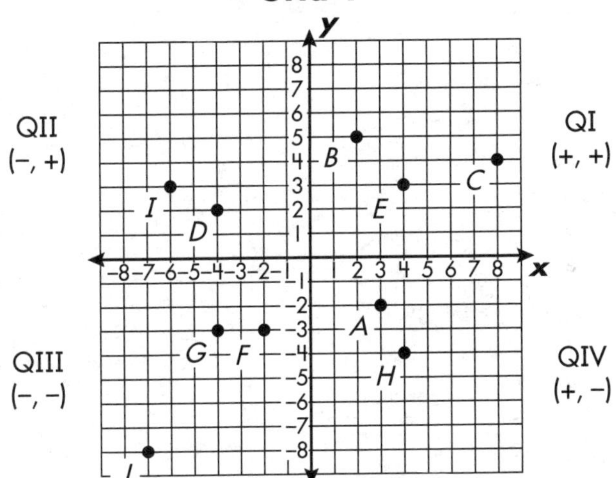

14.

Day	Amount Spent (Dollars)	Amount Saved
Mon	58.00	5.80
Tues	88.50	8.85
Wed	28.60	2.86
Thurs	72.20	3.61
Fri	94.00	4.70
Sat	46.77	2.34
Sun	39.00	1.95

Groceries: Amount Spent and Amount Saved

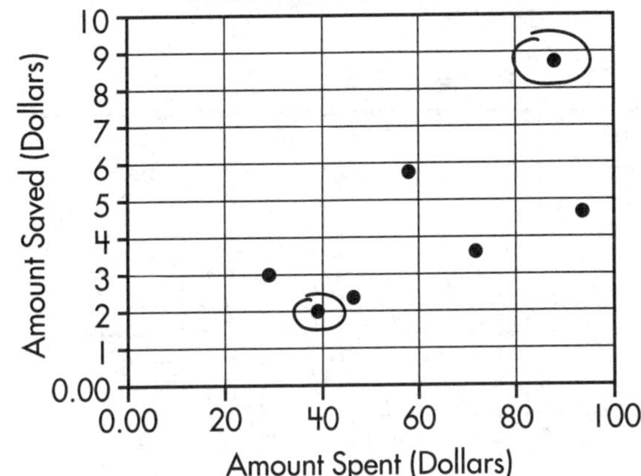

Mid-Test, Page 47

	a	b	c	d
1.	$2\frac{1}{8}$	$\frac{8}{15}$	$\frac{3}{128}$	$12\frac{3}{22}$
2.	9.87	4.22	21.45	71.82
3.	16	51.90128	17.6	$11\frac{31}{80}$

4. $18\frac{5}{12}$

5. $9,017.03

6. 8

Mid-Test, Page 48

	a	b
7.	4; *x*	2; *d*
8.	(4 + 1); 2	(10 – 2); 38
9.	commutative	zero
10.	associative	identity
11.	22	0
12.	(5*x* + *a*) + *b*	*b* + *n*
13.	10 × (*a* + *b*)	(*a* × *d*) + (*a* × *b*)
14.	9	8

Data Analysis and Probability Answers

	a	b	c
15.	16	100	126
16.	35	93	304
17.	3	1620	1496
18.	192	3	7

Mid-Test, Page 49

19. 122 – n = 12; 110
20. 88 ÷ n = 8 or 88 ÷ 8 = n; 11
21. 15,762
22. January and February
23. 11,386 + n = 15,762; 4,376

	a	b	c
24.	2	3	9
25.	24	28	182

Mid-Test, Page 50

26.	–1	3	15
27.	20	–12	–96

28-32.

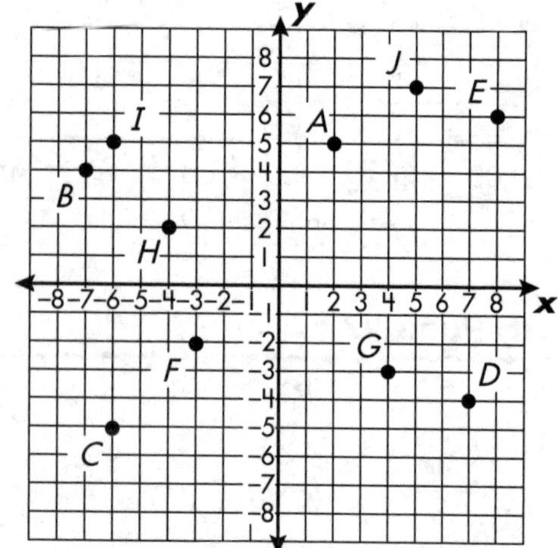

33.

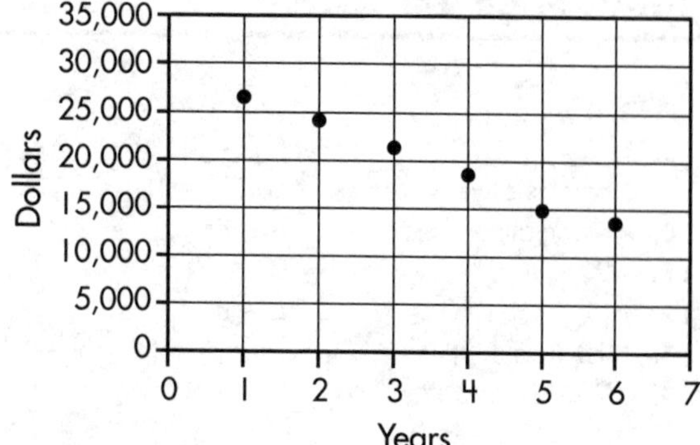

34. $30,000
35. year 1

Chapter 4

Check What You Know, page 51

1. 5
2. $\frac{1}{5}$
3. $\frac{3}{5}$
4. $\frac{2}{5}$
5. $\frac{2}{5}$
6. $\frac{4}{5}$
7. $\frac{2}{9}$
8. $\frac{7}{9}$
9. $\frac{2}{3}$
10. 0

Check What You Know, page 52

11. $\frac{1}{7}$
12. $\frac{2}{21}$
13. $\frac{4}{15}$
14. $\frac{1}{5}$
15. 8
16. $\frac{1}{8}$
17. $\frac{1}{64}$

Lesson 4.1, page 53

1. $\frac{1}{2}$
2. $\frac{1}{3}$
3. $\frac{1}{6}$
4. $\frac{1}{3}$
5. $\frac{1}{6}$
6. $\frac{1}{6}$
7. $\frac{1}{3}$
8. 0

Lesson 4.1, page 54

1. $\frac{2}{3}$
2. $\frac{5}{8}$
3. $\frac{1}{2}$
4. $\frac{3}{8}$

Lesson 4.1, page 55

1. $\frac{6}{35}$
2. $\frac{9}{25}$
3. $\frac{1}{4}$
4. $\frac{9}{64}$

Data Analysis and Probability Answers

Lesson 4.1, page 56

1. $\frac{1}{8}$
2. $\frac{9}{10}$
3. $\frac{1}{10}$
4. $\frac{1}{220}$

Lesson 4.2, page 57

1. 12

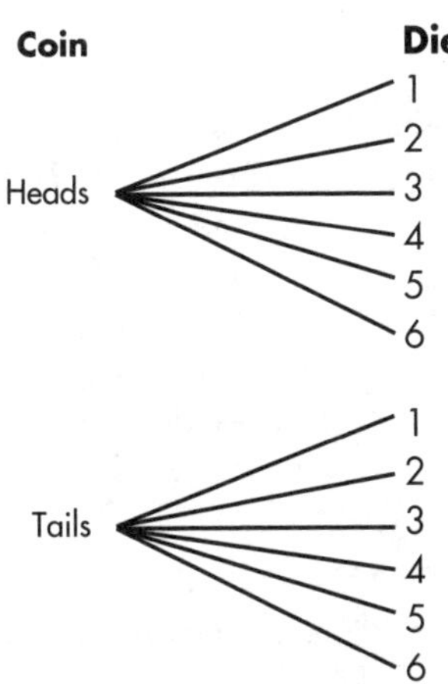

Lesson 4.2, page 58

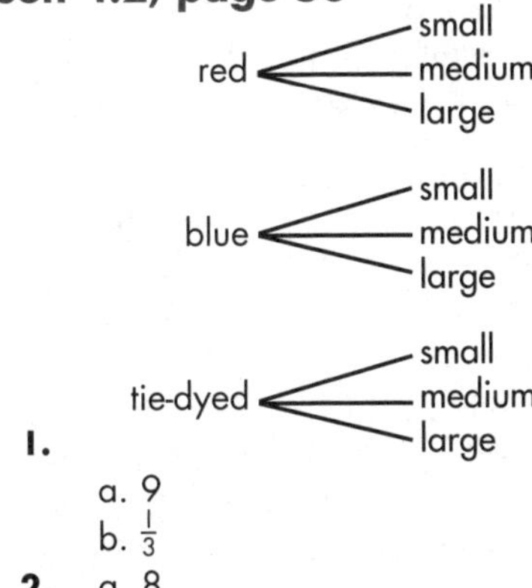

1.
   a. 9
   b. $\frac{1}{3}$
2.
   a. 8
   b. $\frac{1}{2}$
   c. $\frac{1}{4}$
   d. $\frac{1}{8}$

Lesson 4.3, page 59

1. $\frac{1}{6}$
2. $\frac{1}{3}$
3. $\frac{5}{6}$
4. $\frac{1}{36}$
5. $\frac{1}{5}$
6. $\frac{7}{10}$
7. $\frac{2}{15}$
8. $\frac{13}{15}$

Lesson 4.3, page 60

1. **CHART**

Coin

Spinner	Heads	Tails
1	H1	T1
2	H2	T2
3	H3	T3
4	H4	T4

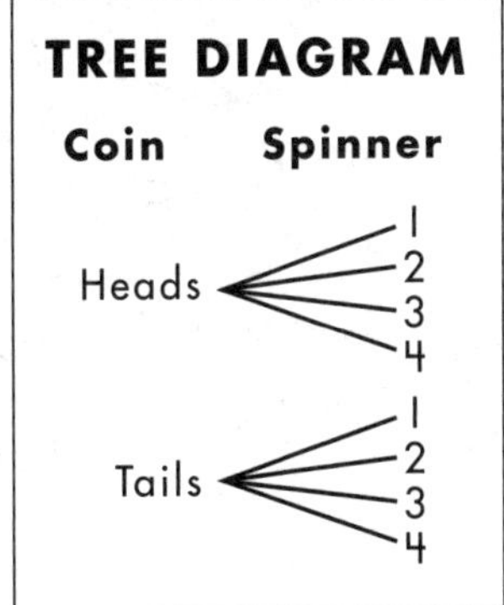

2. 8
3. 12.5%
4. 87.5%
5. 25%

Check What You Learned, page 61

1. $\frac{1}{13}$
2. $\frac{1}{4}$
3. $\frac{17}{52}$
4. $\frac{3}{4}$
5. $\frac{1}{169}$
6. $\frac{1}{16}$
7. $\frac{1}{52}$
8. $\frac{4}{663}$
9. $\frac{13}{204}$

Data Analysis and Probability Answers

Check What You Learned, page 62

10. $\frac{5}{57}$
11. $\frac{20}{171}$
12.

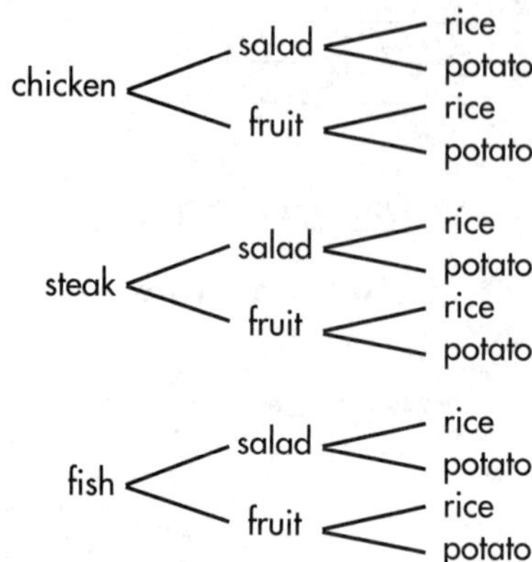

13. 12
14. 50%
15. 16.7%
16. 8.3%

Chapter 5

Check What You Know, page 63

		a	b	c
1.	mean:	6.4	21	3.5
	median:	8	20.5	3.5
	mode:	9	17	none
	range:	7	15	7

2. a. $\frac{80+86+79+81+n}{5} = 84$
b. 94
3. a. $\frac{720}{n} = 24$
b. 30
4. 32, 35, 37
5. 61
6. 44
7. 21
8. 40

Check What You Know, page 64

9.

Popularity of Colors for Cars			
Color	Frequency	Cumulative Frequency	Relative Frequency
red	25	25	17.9%
blue	20	45	14.3%
black	16	61	11.4%
silver	43	104	30.7%
white	36	140	25.7%

10. 140
11. silver
12. 40%
13. 7
14. 8
15. 20
16. 7.5
17. 12
18. 14
19. 8

Lesson 5.1, page 65

	a	b
1.	mean: 20	mean: $27\frac{1}{2}$
	median: 20	median: $26\frac{1}{2}$
	mode: 25	mode: 21, 36
2.	mean: 17	mean: $18\frac{1}{2}$
	median: 8	median: 5
	mode: none	mode: 0

Lesson 5.1, page 66

1. 81, 84, 88, 93, 97
mean: 88.6; median: 88; mode: none; range: 16
2. 83, 84, 84, 85, 86
mean: 84.4; median: 84; mode: 84; range: 3
3. 85, 88, 90, 92, 92
mean: 89.4; median: 90; mode: 92; range: 7
4. Kara, because her scores had the smallest range

Lesson 5.1, page 67

	a	b
1.	\$9.41	\$9.75
2.	\$9.50	\$8.25
3.	\$9.50; \$10	\$8

4. Sam's Pet World pays better. The \$20 wage in the set for Beth's Pets is an outlier that increases the mean above Sam's. However, the higher median and mode show that most of Sam's employees are paid better.
5. the mean, because it provides the highest value for this set of wages

Lesson 5.1, page 68

1. 17
2. 34
3. \$285

Data Analysis and Probability Answers

Lesson 5.2, page 69

Pet Ownership				
Number of Pets	Frequency	Cumulative Frequency	Relative Frequency (fraction)	Relative Frequency (percent)
0	8	8	$\frac{2}{15}$	13.3%
1	29	37	$\frac{29}{60}$	48.3%
2	15	52	$\frac{1}{4}$	25.0%
3	6	58	$\frac{1}{10}$	10%
4+	2	60	$\frac{1}{30}$	3.3%

1. 60
2. $\frac{7}{20}$

Lesson 5.2, page 70

Points Scored per Basketball Game			
Points	Frequency	Cumulative Frequency	Relative Frequency
30–39	3	3	$\frac{1}{10}$
40–49	5	8	$\frac{1}{6}$
50–59	8	16	$\frac{4}{15}$
60–69	10	26	$\frac{1}{3}$
70–79	4	30	$\frac{2}{15}$

1. 30
2. 10
3. 4.6, 4.6, 4.8, 5.1, 5.2, 5.2, 5.2, 5.3, 5.4, 5.4, 5.4, 5.5, 5.6, 5.6, 5.7, 5.8, 5.9, 5.9, 6.0, 6.1

Heights of Students in a Class			
Height, in Feet	Frequency	Cumulative Frequency	Relative Frequency
4.5–4.9	3	3	15%
5.0–5.4	8	11	40%
5.5–5.9	7	18	35%
6.0–6.5	2	20	10%

4. 20
5. 5.0–5.4
6. 10%
7. 90%

Lesson 5.3, page 71

1. 73, 91
2. 115
3. 73
4. 42

Lesson 5.3, page 72

1. Keys will vary. Example: 3 | 1 = 31

Stem	Leaves
2	2 6 7 9 9
3	1 2 5
4	4 6 6
5	3 5

2. Keys will vary. Example: 43 | 5 = 435

Stem	Leaves
43	2 5
44	1 2 3
45	1 1 5 5
46	9 9

3. Keys will vary. Example: 5 | 9 = 59

Stem	Leaves
4	0 6 9
5	2 6 6 9 9 9
6	0 0 0 2 3 3 3 3 4 8
7	0 0 2 4 4 6 6
8	0 1 2 3

4. 63 degrees
5. 43 degrees
6. 63 degrees

Lesson 5.4, page 73

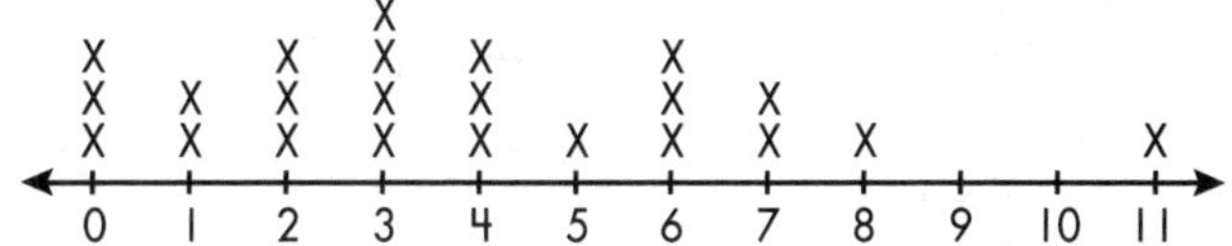

1. 3; 11
2. 23; 3
3. 11

Lesson 5.4, page 74

1. 56 and 57
2. 25
3. 26
4. 56.5
5. Sample answer: from 54 through 60 transactions, because most clerks have been performing within this cluster of transactions
6. Sample answer: above 65 transactions, because a number beyond 65 would be an outlier, indicating an exceptionally high number of transactions

Data Analysis and Probability Answers

Lesson 5.5, page 75

1. 50
2. 10
3. 40
4. 20
5. 25
6. 10; 35
7.

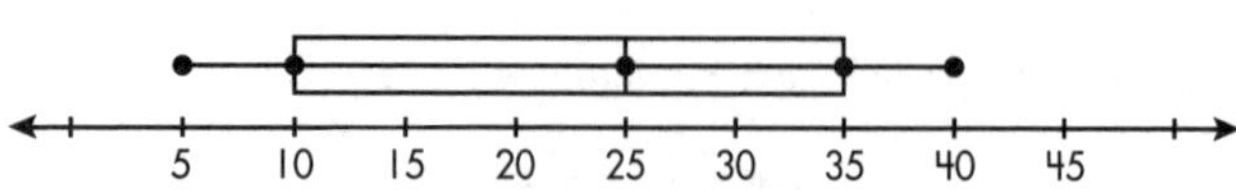

Lesson 5.5, page 76

1. 14
2. 7
3. \$15; \$24
4. top 50%; the distance from the median to the upper extreme appears greater than to the lower extreme
5. 300
6. 150
7. yes, because 50% of flights carry 300 or more passengers, and planes this size could be responsible for some of the flights carrying fewer than 300

Lesson 5.6, page 77

1. 247
2. 280
3. 250
4. 239
5. 280
6. 250
7. mean
8. The mean would increase.
9. The mode would not change.
10. The median would not change.
11. 250
12. 280

Lesson 5.6, page 78

1. Seattle
   a. Seattle's interquartile range and overall range span a narrow set of mild temperatures.
   b. Seattle's temperatures cluster compactly in a mild range.
2. Cleveland
   a. Cleveland has wider ranges and extremes.
   b. Cleveland has temperature clusters at the low end and at the higher end.
3. stem-and-leaf (means cannot be determined from box-and whisker plots)
4. probably box-and-whisker because the median is marked, but some students might prefer using the actual data provided in the stem-and-leaf plot
5. stem-and-leaf (modes cannot be determined from box-and whisker plots)
6. probably box-and-whisker because of its visual representation, but some students might prefer to consider the data clustering provided by the stem-and-leaf in their analysis of spread

Check What You Learned, page 79

		a	b	c
1.	mean:	22.8	28.7	9.1
	median:	20	15	8
	mode:	18	0	3, 4, 12
	range:	41	113	17

2. mean
3. a. $\frac{24 + 20 + 26 + 14 + 18 + n}{6} = 20$
   b. 18
4. a. $\frac{n}{24} = 65$
   b. 1,560
5. Keys will vary. Example: 22 | 7 = 227

Stem	Leaves
22	2 7
23	5 6 9
24	3 4
25	1 6
26	0 7

6. none
7. 243
8. 222
9. 45

Check What You Learned, page 80

10.

Minutes	Frequency	Cumulative Frequency	Relative Frequency
30–34	4	4	26.7%
35–39	2	6	13.3%
40–44	7	13	46.7%
45–49	2	15	13.3%

11.

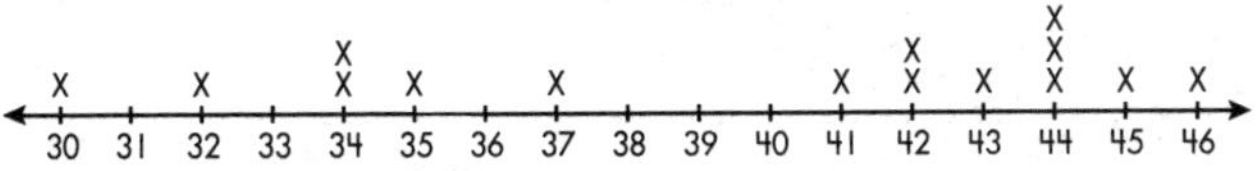

12.

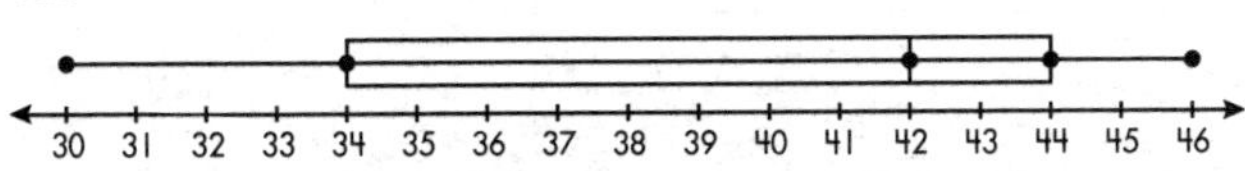

	a	b
13.	39.5	16
14.	42	46
15.	44	30
16.	34	10

Chapter 6

Check What You Know, page 81

1.

Annual Product Exports			
Country	**Sales (millions)**	**%**	**Degrees**
Germany	$12	24%	86.4°
Great Britain	16	32%	115.2°
France	10	20%	72.0°
Canada	7	14%	50.4°
China	4	8%	28.8°
Korea	1	2%	7.2°
Total:	**$50**	**100%**	**360°**

Annual Product Exports
Total: $50 Million

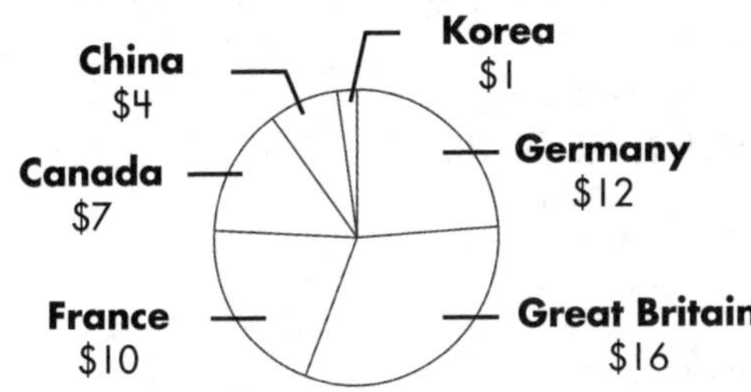

2. investment dollars by age group
3. a 15-year age group
4. 65–80 age group
5. investment dollars, in millions
6. 80–95 age group

Data Analysis and Probability Answers

Check What You Know, page 82

7.

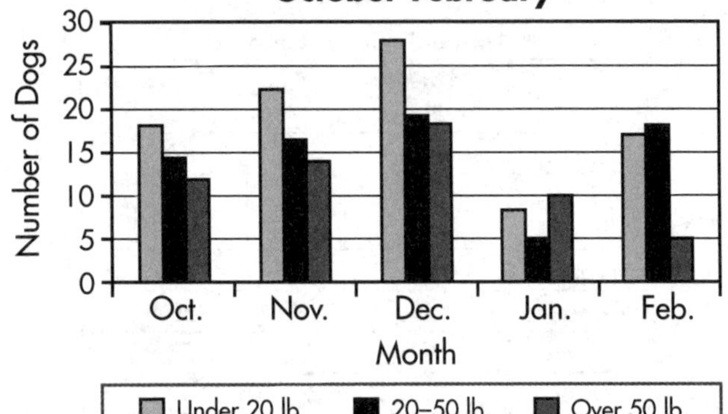

8. the number of new dog arrivals and adoptions from October–February
9. November and January
10. the age of homes and their selling price
11. no
12. no correlation

Lesson 6.1, page 83

1. June; February
2. 1,727; 66.8%
3. 857; 33.2%

Lesson 6.1, page 84

1. units sold over $400, units sold $200–399, and units sold under $200
2. a. units over $400 b. 675
3. 21.1%

Lesson 6.2, page 85

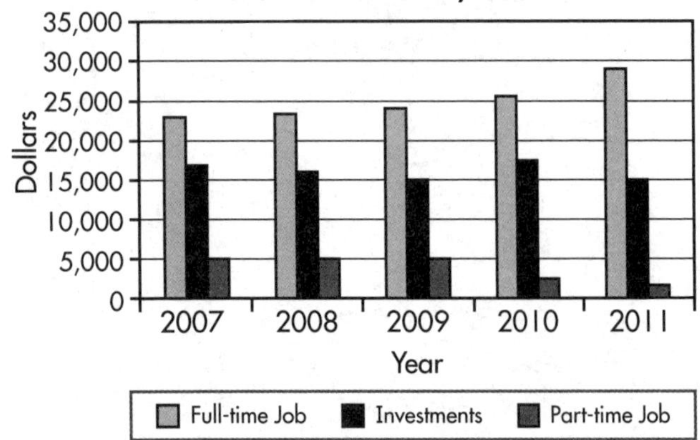

1. $44,767; $44,604
2. $22,745; $28,972
3. His other sources of income decreased.

Lesson 6.3, page 86

1. 11.5–12.0
2. 11–11.5
3. number of employees
4. driving miles
5. 72
6. 31

Lesson 6.4, page 87

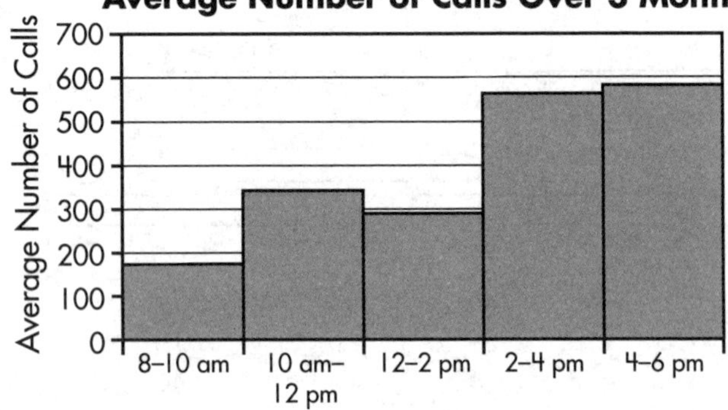

1. time periods; average number of calls
2. 100
3. 10 am–12 pm, 2–4 pm, 4–6 pm

Lesson 6.5, page 88

1. academic year enrollment
2. an increase in enrollment
3. Enrollment is flat from 2008–2009 to 2009–2010.
4. 32% increase
5. 3,605

Lesson 6.5, page 89

1. Venice
2. Miami
3. Plant A: Week 4; Plant B: Week 3; Plant C: Week 5
4. Plant C

Data Analysis and Probability Answers

Lesson 6.6, page 90

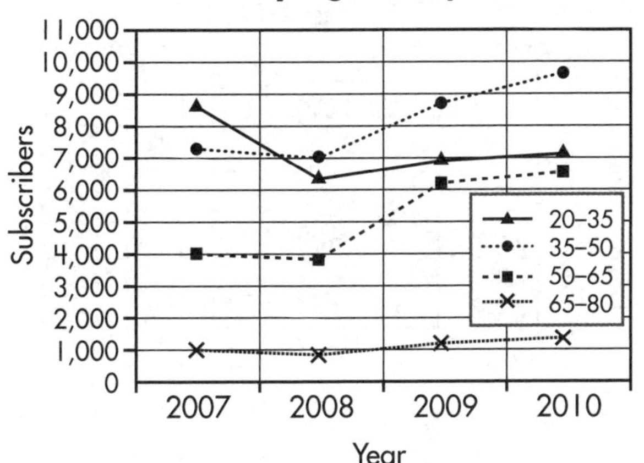

1. 20–35 age group; 65–80 age group
2. 2008
3. 35–50 and 50–65 age groups

Lesson 6.7, page 91

1. Sector A: 40% or 144°
2. Sector B: 10% or 36°
3. Sector C: 30% or 108°
4. Sector D: 20% or 72°
5.

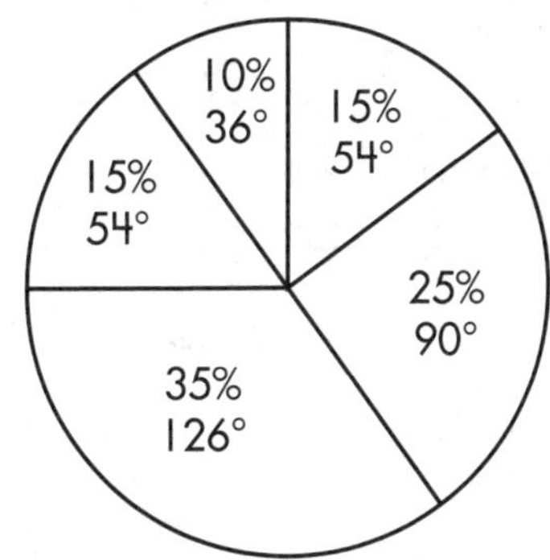

Lesson 6.7, page 92

1.

Income Source	Percent
Property Tax	58.2%
Interest from Reserve Fund	9.2%
Sales Tax	17.4%
Permits and Fees	5.1%
Fines	2.2%
State Grants	4.4%
Federal Grants	3.5%

2. property tax
3. 7.9%
4. more income than expenses: $1,184,515

Lesson 6.8, page 93

1.

Activity	Percent of 24-Hr. Day
Sleep	35
Work	40
Reading	3
Errands & Housework	5
Friends & Family	1.5
Hobbies & TV	13.3
Meals	2.2

Kassie Lewis
Hours Spent on Daily Activities

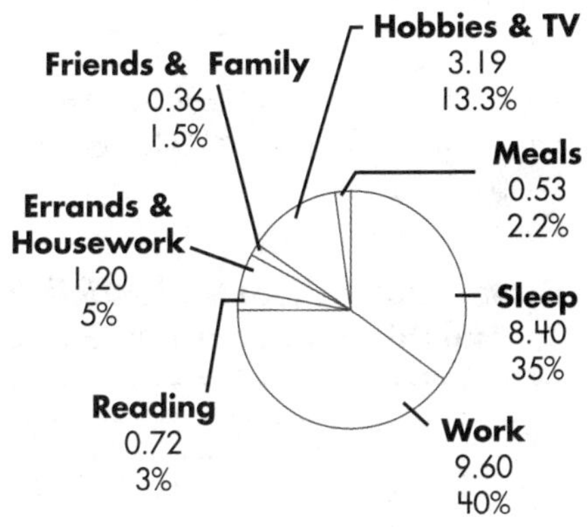

2. about 22 min.
3. 13.3%

Lesson 6.9, page 94

Barker Real Estate Sales Agents and Units Sold

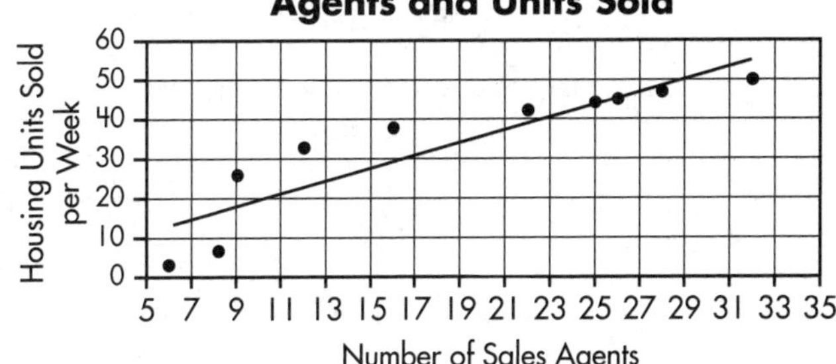

1. number of sales agents (*x* axis) to housing units sold per week (*y* axis)
2. As the number of sales agents increases, the housing units sold per week increase.

Data Analysis and Probability Answers

Lesson 6.9, page 95

1. outlier
2. negative correlation
3. Sales of those pictures would increase.

Lesson 6.10, page 96

1.

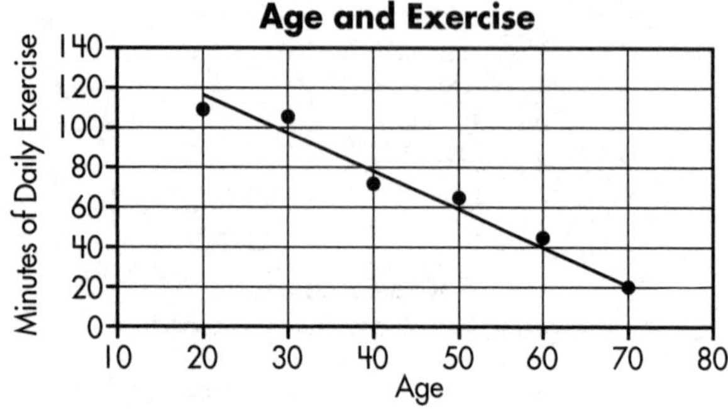

2. The scatterplot shows a negative correlation. As age increases, minutes of daily exercise decrease.
3. 0–20 min. per day
4. there is no correlation

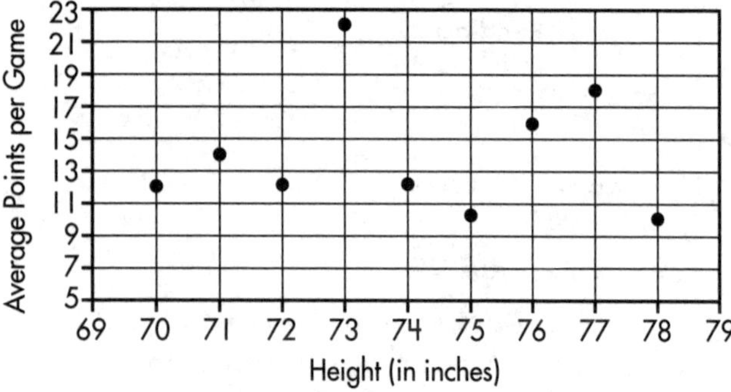

The scatterplot does not show a correlation.

Lesson 6.11, page 97

1.

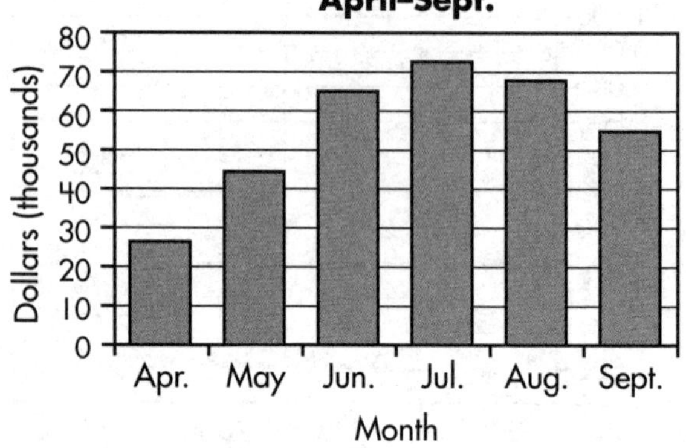

2. July
3. a. Jackson, b. Willow, c. Tramore, d. 18

Lesson 6.11, page 98

4. a. $1,800 b. 37.9%
5. a. January, May, June b. February, March
6. between 2.5 and 2.6 lbs.

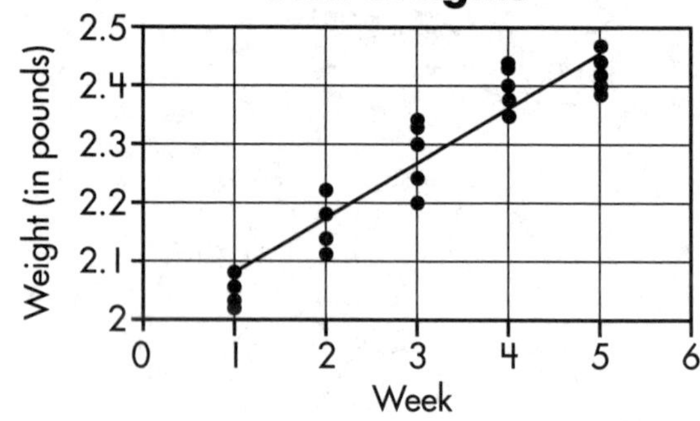

Data Analysis and Probability Answers

Check What You Learned, page 99

1.

Tina's Gifts Annual Sales			
Item	**Sales**	**%**	**Degrees**
Music	$30,876	24.1%	86.8°
Books	$22,245	17.4%	62.6°
Jewelry	$37,890	29.6%	106.6°
Cards	$4,200	3.3%	11.9°
Clothing	$12,789	10%	36°
Shoes	$16,740	13.1%	47.2°
Perfume	$3,200	2.5%	9°
Total:	**$127,940**	100%	360°

Tina's Gifts Annual Sales

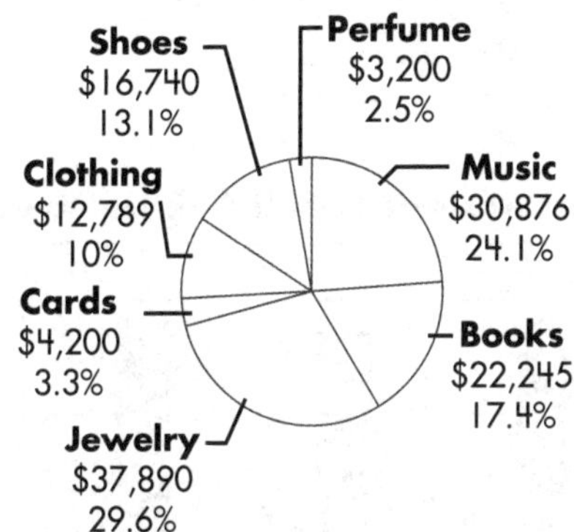

2. unit sales for four types of instruments from Sept. to Dec.
3. percussion, brass
4. brass; Dec.
5. Dec.

Check What You Learned, page 100

6.

Vehicles per Hour

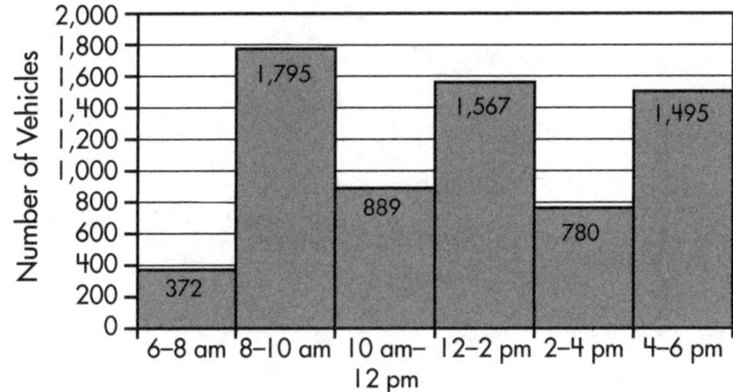

7. regular
8. 8–10 am
9. number of cars and gallons of gas sold

Traffic Volume and Gallons Sold

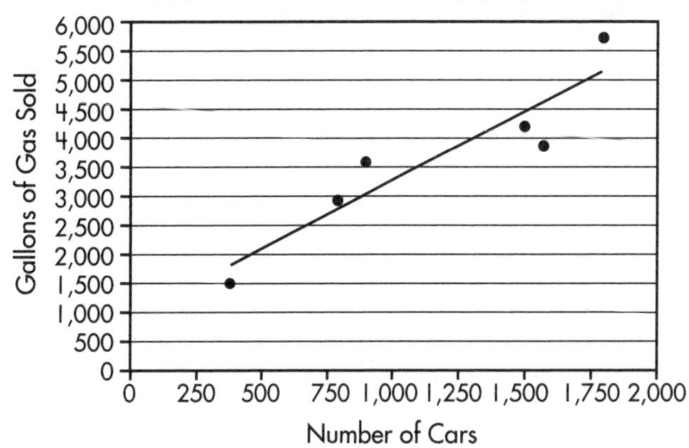

10. positive correlation

Final Test, Page 101

	a	b	c	d
1.	$3\frac{7}{32}$	$3\frac{5}{8}$	$\frac{1}{30}$	$4\frac{8}{11}$
2.	6.86	4.21	11.44	18.3

3. $7\frac{1}{6}$
4. $2,109.90
5. 22
6. $364.50

Final Test, Page 102

	a	b
7.	(3 + 2); 3	(14 – 8); 16
8.	8 ÷ 2; 14	(4 – 2); 16
9.	associative	identity
10.	commutative	zero
11.	$(a \times 7) - (2 \times 7)$;	$(k \times m) + (k \times n)$

	a	b	c
12.	24	136	158
13.	36	15	94

14. $222 - n = 46$; 176
15. $158 - (16 \times 3) = n$; 110

Data Analysis and Probability Answers

Final Test, Page 103

	a	b	c
16.	2	32	64
17.	35	104	44

18-22.

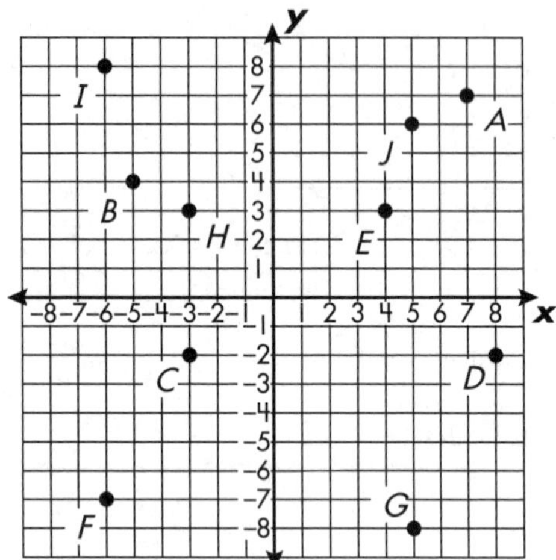

23. 6
24. $\frac{1}{6}$
25. $\frac{1}{2}$
26. $\frac{1}{2}$
27. $\frac{1}{6}$
28. $\frac{11}{16}$

Final Test, Page 104

29. $\frac{1}{12}$
30. $\frac{20}{77}$

	a	b	c
31.	mean: 9.2 median: 8 mode: 8 range: 5	mean: 22.7 median: 22.5 mode: none range: 18	mean: 10.25 median: 12 mode: 13 range: 15

32.

Customer Service Calls			
Number of Calls	Frequency	Cumulative Frequency	Relative Frequency
0–49	16	16	7.0%
50–99	48	64	21.1%
100–149	57	121	25.1%
150–199	60	181	26.4%
200–250	46	227	20.3%

33. 60
34. 7%

Final Test, Page 105

35. 4
36. 8
37. 4.5
38. 24
39. sources of Jan Farmer's 2010 income
40. her full-time job
41. Jan Farmer's income, expenses, and savings, 2007–2011
42. 2008
43. 2011
44. 2008–2011

Final Test, Page 106

45. year 2
46. 5,300
47. positive
48.

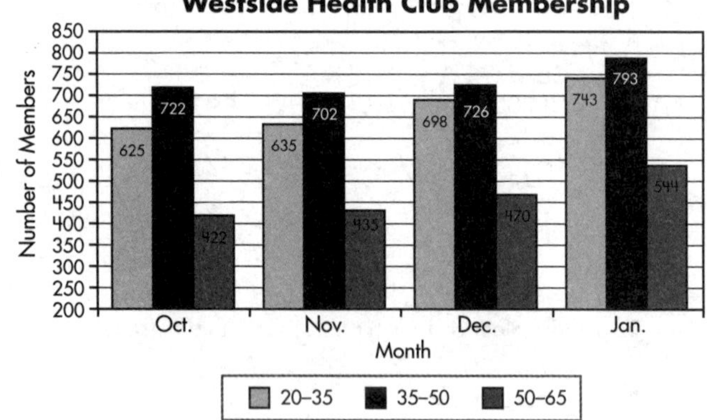

49. 35–50; 50–65
50. 50–65